The Suffering Question

The Suffering Question

Biblical Insights Into

Why **Bad Things** Happen to *Good People*

by

Mac Hammond

The Suffering Question—
Biblical Insights Into Why Bad Things Happen to Good People

ISBN 978-1-57399-409-5
Copyright © 2009 by Mac Hammond

Published by Mac Hammond Ministries
PO Box 29469
Minneapolis, MN 55429

Contents

Forward 1

Part One
The Suffering Question

Chapter 1
Building Your Life on a Strong Foundation 5

Chapter 2
Who God Is 9

Chapter 3
What About Job? 13

Part 2
Taking Job Apart

Chapter 4
Job's Limitations 23

Chapter 5
Job's Calamities 27

Chapter 6
Job's Debate 39

Chapter 7
The "Wisdom" of Job 45

Chapter 8
Turning Job Around 51

Part 3
Putting Job Back Together

Chapter 9
Steps Toward Deliverance 57

Part 4
Redefining Suffering

Chapter 10
Do Christians Have to Suffer at All? 69

Chapter 11
Persecution for Jesus' Sake 77

Chapter 12
The Suffering of Consecration 81

Part 5
Breezing Through the Storms of Life

Chapter 13
Facing the Storms of Life 89

Chapter 14
Storms of Various Kinds 95

Chapter 15
Who You Are in Christ 99

Chapter 16
Abiding in the Vine 105

Conclusion 111

Endnotes 112

References 113

Forward

"Mother, Son Slain in South Minneapolis." "Millions Flee Chinese Floods." "Tornado Kills Four in Iowa Boy Scout Camp."

Watching the nightly news can be depressing. So much hurt and pain fills the world today, and it seems like every day brings something else—a new strain of the flu bug, the latest terrorist threat, another hurricane.

Why? Why is there so much suffering in the world? If there really is a loving God, why do these things happen?

People all over the world have asked these types of questions for centuries. They've hypothesized, drawn conclusions, and created theories about why bad things happen, especially to good people.

More often than not, God gets blamed for the suffering. In fact, the topic of human suffering does more to shape theological perspective than any other single factor, for both believers and unbelievers alike. Unbelievers say, "If there really is a God..." or "If God really cared, this world wouldn't be in such a mess." Believers say, "God's trying to teach me a lesson" or "God is punishing me for my mistakes."

The consistent message of the Bible goes against these conclusions. The Bible shows us that God doesn't send us evil in any way, shape, or form. Time and again, we're told God wants us to be blessed (Psalm 35:27, Deuteronomy 28:1–14); He's made provision for our blessing (2 Corinthians 9:8, Galatians 3:14); and He wants us to have life as He has it (Psalm 36:7–8, 2 Peter 1:3–4).

But when people go through tragic circumstances, they often become confused. They hear that God wants good for them, but then they watch someone die prematurely, or see a Christian pray for healing and stay sick, or hear about a national disaster that has occurred. They begin to wonder, *Why did God let that happen?*

Usually around that time, they hear someone who is steeped in religious tradition talk about the suffering of Job or the thorn in Paul's flesh. They might even hear someone reference the Old Testament verses that seem to say the Lord brings destruction on people. And that's when the issue begins to appear murky. The Bible says God wants good for us, but it seems to be saying that He brings suffering into our lives as well.

Can both of these thoughts be true?

The Big Picture

Well, imagine for a moment that you had a thousand-piece puzzle scattered on your living room floor, but someone threw away the box top. Would you want to even attempt to put the puzzle together? Sure, you could put it together by matching up the colors and shapes of each piece to create the full picture, but it would take hours and possibly never get done. It's much easier to put the puzzle together when you have the box top. Why? Because when you can see the whole picture, the smaller pieces fall into place much more quickly.

In the same way, the questions people have about suffering have answers, but they are very different from the traditional religious perspective. It's the big picture that will help you put all the pieces together in a way that makes sense and is biblically accurate.

And that's what I want to show you in this book—a consistent, clear picture about who God is and what we can expect from Him, especially as it relates to suffering.

Be prepared to throw preconceived ideas out the window. Let go of religious mindsets that may bog you down. Let's take a journey through the bigger picture of why people suffer.

The
Suffering
Question

Part 1

Building Your Life on a Strong Foundation

If given the option, what would you prefer to build a house on—sand or rock?

I know. It's a pretty obvious option. People do not willingly choose to build their houses upon sand. People instinctively know that if the foundation of the house is unstable, the whole house will be unstable.

As simple as that truth is, a lot of people dismiss its importance with regard to their relationship with God. They don't realize that what they think about God will be the foundation for every other belief in their lives. If they have a skewed view of Him, the rest of their lives will be affected by that unstable foundation.

I'm reminded of a story of a Christian man who once starved to death in his pickup in the mountains of Oregon. Stuck in a snow drift in a mountain pass, he sat in his truck for nine weeks, waiting for someone to rescue him "if it was the Lord's will."

During that time, he kept a diary and wrote letters to loved ones. It's clear from his writings that he believed God had caused him to get stuck in the snow and that he would get out only if God wanted him to.

For more than two months, he sat in his truck wondering whether it was God's will for him to live. Finally, he died of starvation. Someone found his body, a hundred yards from a clear road he could have used to find help. One hundred yards of snow and a wrong idea about God stood between this man and life.

Starvation didn't kill him. His theology did.

Our view of God is truly that important. If we don't build our lives on a correct view of God, we may wind up like that man did—spiritually wasting away due to limited knowledge about God.

Built on a Rock

Jesus knew the importance of this truth. That's why He asked His disciples in Matthew 16:13, "Who are people saying that I am?" They responded, "Some say you're John the Baptist, some Elias, others Jeremiah." Then Jesus said to them:

> *"But who do you say that I am?" Simon Peter answered and said, "You are the Christ, the Son of the living God." Jesus answered and said to him, "Blessed are you, Simon Bar-Jonah, for flesh and blood has not revealed this to you, but My Father who is in heaven. And I also say to you that you are Peter, and on this rock I will build My church, and the gates of Hades shall not prevail against it* (Matthew 16:15–18 NKJV).

What is the rock that Jesus said He would build His Church upon? Some religious circles believe it was the apostle Peter, but I disagree with that conclusion. True, Peter was a great man of God, but it seems unlikely that God would build His Church on someone who was just as human as any of us.

Jesus must have been talking about a different rock.

Look back to how the conversation started. Jesus asked, "Whom do you say I am?" Peter said, "You are the Christ, the Son of the Living God." Peter knew who Jesus was. It wasn't something he came up with on his own; it was a revelation God gave him. Because of that revelation, Jesus was able to say, "Upon this rock [the rock of a clear revelation of who God is] I will build My church; and the gates of hell shall not prevail against it."

What Jesus is saying here is that to the extent that you and I, as members of His Church, have a clear, unclouded revelation of who God is, our lives will be built on solid rock, just as Peter's was. Ultimately, as we each build a solid, unshakeable understanding of who God is, the gates of hell will not be able to prevail against us.

The Greatest Obstacle to Understanding God

I want you to notice that verse 19 continues with the word "and":

And I will give you the keys of the kingdom of heaven, and whatever you bind on earth will be bound in heaven, and whatever you loose on earth will be loosed in heaven" (Matthew 16:19 NKJV).

Who is God giving the keys of the kingdom of heaven to? He's giving them to the people who have a clear revelation of who He is.

Your revelation of who God is determines how your life is built in God. It determines whether or not the keys of the kingdom will be yours. It determines whether or not what you bind stays bound or what you loose stays loosed.

And that's why it's important to understand what is the single greatest obstacle to a clear revelation of who God is…

It is the suffering question.

When faced with the question, "Does God make people suffer?" most people look to natural circumstances, past situations, or faulty teachings for the answer. But, in reality, none of these things will ever and can never present a clear view of who God is.

The only place we can come to a clear view about God is by looking at His Word. By studying God's Word, we can know His character. And when we know His character, we can know how He'll act in any given situation.

For example, if someone was accused of stealing, you may be inclined to agree with the accuser if there was enough evidence and if you didn't know the accused person that well. But if one of your good friends was accused of stealing, you'd come to your friend's defense because you know that your friend would never steal anything.

This same principle is true with God. Suffering is a reality in today's world. Does that mean God has a part in it? If you don't know Him that well, you may be inclined to think He is connected with it. On the other hand, if you know Him and His character, you know that in no way is He connected with any type of suffering.

So what is God's nature? That's what I want to show you in the next chapter, because when you know what God's nature is, you'll be better positioned to answer the suffering question in a way that is biblically accurate.

Who God Is

Who is God? How can we expect Him to act? If you and I spent the rest of our lives trying to answer these questions, we would only scratch the surface! What I can do is point out a few characteristics of God's nature that are important for us to identify before we study why people suffer.

Malachi 3:6 (NKJV) reveals to us an important characteristic of God, one that you should keep in the back of your mind throughout this entire book. It says:

> For I am the Lord, I do not change; therefore you are not consumed, O sons of Jacob.

God will not change. He's "the same yesterday, today, and for ever" (Hebrews 13:8). In Him is "no variableness, neither shadow of turning" (James 1:17).

God isn't like us. He never wakes up in a bad mood. He doesn't have "off" days or get up on the wrong side of the bed. He doesn't change His mind or alter the way He looks at things. When you find out the truth of how He'll act in one situation, you can expect Him to act that way in similar situations.

Whenever you call on Him, you can know He'll act according to His character—with compassion (Psalm 145:8–9), loving kindness (Psalm 36:7), and mercy (Ephesians 2:4).

The God of the Living

The second characteristic of God's nature I want to show you is in Matthew 22:31–32:

But concerning the resurrection of the dead, have you not read what was spoken to you by God, saying, 'I am the God of Abraham, the God of Isaac, and the God of Jacob'? God is not the God of the dead, but of the living" (NKJV).

God doesn't deal with death. He doesn't work with anything that contributes to death of any sort. His only method of working is with life.

How should that affect your understanding of who He is? Anything that contributes to death in your experience of life is not from God.

Sickness is a form of death. Poverty is a form of death. Anger, strife, and relational problems all lead to death— maybe not physical death, but certainly, the death of a relationship, of hope, or of security.

God has no part in any of these things. He brings His children out of any form of death, not into it. This is a simple, yet important, truth that must be understood when looking to answer the suffering question.

Confusion? Not From God

What else can we know about God? Paul wrote in 1 Corinthians 14:33:

For God is not the author of confusion but of peace, as in all the churches of the saints (NKJV).

That word *confusion* literally means "disorder." It also can refer to chaos.[1] When you are in a gathering, particularly a church gathering, that is disorderly or chaotic, God isn't organizing it. He is the one who makes order out of chaos. He doesn't deal with the confusion that comes from chaos. Instead, He brings peace.

The word *peace* literally means "prosperity."[2] Prosperity is a reference not just to financial increase but

The Suffering Question

to the increase of every good thing—joy, good relationships, a healthy body, etc. It is the antithesis of disorder and confusion.

Sickness, disease, terrorism, famines, and natural disasters—none of these things bring order, peace, or prosperity. In fact, they bring the exact opposite. And God has no part in that type of confusion. As Paul says, God is the God of peace (Philippians 4:9, 1 Thessalonians 5:23).

Understanding God

I could show you a lot more characteristics of God's nature, but I think you get the idea. God deals with life and victory, not death and suffering. That's what you can expect from Him. No matter what question you come across, no matter what suffering you or others face, God is not behind death or things related to death. The enemy is. And I want to spend the rest of this book refuting some of the theories that have so often clouded people's views of who God truly is.

One reason I want you to know how to answer the suffering question is because if you've bought the idea that God is related to or possibly even the author of your chaos and confusion, you'll accept your circumstances as they are and assume there is nothing you can do about them. You won't resist Satan effectively if you feel God may be connected with it.

On the other hand, if you know who God is and you know how He acts, the very gates of hell will not be able to prevail against you, because you have a proper view of both God and your enemy, Satan.

The Believer's Point of View

I'll be answering the suffering question specifically from the believer's perspective. I won't take the space to delve into why the unbeliever suffers, except to say that the world remains a mess because men are free moral agents and have chosen their ways over God's ways ever since Adam disobeyed God's command in the Garden of Eden. God won't impose His will on unbelievers (or believers, for that matter), even if it would be in their best interests.

On the other hand, believers who are doing their best to follow God still suffer tragedy at times. Because of that, many religious teachers cling to the idea that God must be the author of tragedy. If God doesn't stop something bad from happening or answer a problem as they expect Him to, they often assume He must be the one who brings the suffering.

I find this mindset slightly strange. Why do Christians who believe God sent His own Son to die on the cross for their sins have a tough time believing God wants good things for them, not bad? That's hard for me to understand.

There must be an answer to the suffering question—one that's consistent with God and His nature. Let's find out what it is.

What About Job?

All of us would probably agree that the person in the Bible most often associated with suffering is Job. "Poor old Job. He had such a hard life. And he's our example. We must suffer like Job did."

People associate trials, tribulations, and hardships with Job, usually with the idea that those things are divinely imposed. Religious scholars claim the book of Job reveals why the righteous suffer. Both draw the conclusion that Job's story shows us how God uses hardship to shape our lives in a way that is beyond our natural understanding.

But contrary to popular opinion, these mindsets are terrible misconceptions. They go against the very character of God, as we studied in the last chapter.

People draw these conclusions without having a good knowledge of the book of Job. I've asked my congregation, "How many of you have read Job through from front to back? How many of you are completely satisfied, you have no problems with it, and you understand it completely?" These questions draw a laugh, but never a show of hands.

I do agree that there are some things in this life we won't understand. There are things in the heart of man that only God can know. (I'm sure you can think of something you know about yourself that no one else, not even your spouse, knows about you.)

In addition, we don't know the whole plan of God. If we knew the full plan of God for our lives, we'd probably rush ahead, take matters into our own hands, and mess it up. As Paul wrote in 1 Corinthians 2:8, if the princes of this world had known better, they wouldn't have crucified the Lord of glory. God knows what information needs to be kept hidden for the time being.

And even though we won't understand everything, I can tell you this. We need to do our best to understand what we *can* know. And truly, it's impossible to have a proper revelation of God without having a proper understanding of the book of Job.

Correctly Interpreting the Bible

Let's lay a bit of groundwork for our study. We need to be mindful of two principles of Bible interpretation before going to the text of Job. (There are other standard rules for rightly dividing the Word of God, but for the sake of space, I'm only going to talk about two of the rules that directly apply to our study.)

The first rule of Bible interpretation is that you've got to be aware of who's doing the talking. How credible is the speaker as a source of information? For example, when reading through the New Testament, would you listen to everything that came out of the mouth of a Pharisee? Of course, you wouldn't. The Pharisees aren't credible sources of information. When the Pharisees called Jesus a blasphemer several times in the Gospel, do we take that as a true statement and make a doctrine out of it? Certainly not.

The Bible is inspired by the Holy Spirit, and as such, it is truly stated. It gives us an accurate account of events that occurred: who said what, who did what to whom. But not every truly stated passage is a statement of truth. You have to consider the source.

Nowhere is it more important to consider "who said what" than in the book of Job. As I'll expound on later, Job and his three friends are unreliable sources of information about God. Everything they said about God isn't necessarily true; a lot of times, they were stating their opinion just as the Pharisees did. Does that make their opinion correct? Not at all. Should we base our beliefs on what they said? Certainly not.

Who Interprets Whom?

The second rule of Bible interpretation that we have to be mindful of while reading Job is the potential danger of something called the "rule of first mention." The rule itself is valid, to be sure; it's based on the immutability of God. Once a truth is established in scripture, even if it's on the first page of Genesis, it holds true for the whole Bible because God never changes. He doesn't have a better idea later; He had the best one the first time around.

The danger with this rule arises when we begin interpreting the New Testament in light of the Old—using marginal revelation to interpret greater revelation. We need to do the opposite: use the greatest light we have to illuminate the subject at hand.

Here's where people run into trouble with the book of Job. It's one of the oldest books of the Bible; in its original form, it was probably written before Genesis. We had Job before we had much else—a preliminary ray of God's light on this earth in written form. The door of heaven was cracked just a bit, so to speak. Since Job, we've received the other books of the Old Testament, the Gospels, Acts, the Epistles, and Revelation. The door has been opened wide for the light of God to flood the earth.

What this means is that Job didn't have a New Testament to look into and discover that Jesus said, "I am come that they might have life, and that they might have it more abundantly" (John 10:10). So when Job made his famous statement, "The Lord giveth, and the Lord taketh away," it was without the benefit of that light.

When we interpret tragedies seen in today's world, we shouldn't use Job's statement and say, "The Lord gave me my house, my car, my job, my health, my wife, my child, and now the Lord has taken them all away." Instead, we should use all the light available to us from the Scriptures to interpret Job. We look at what Jesus said in John 10:10, and say, "Satan is the one who stole from me; God wants to bring me life and life more abundantly."

It is true that as we uncover principles of truth in the Old Testament, they're going to hold true for the whole Bible. But this doesn't mean that later, fuller statements of truth are to be weakened or thrown out because of something we see in the Old Testament. We must use the light of the New Testament to properly interpret what we see in the Old.

Did God Really Do That?

Frankly, we ought to approach the entire Old Testament the way we'll approach Job in this study. All of us can think of Old Testament passages, especially in the King James translation, in which God seems to have brought diseases or catastrophes on people to teach them lessons. For example, Exodus 15:26 says:

> *"If you diligently heed the voice of the Lord your God and do what is right in His sight, give ear to His commandments and keep all His statutes, I will put none of the diseases on you which I have brought on the Egyptians. For I am the Lord who heals you"* (NKJV).

What exactly is this verse saying? It sounds like if you don't obey God or if you tick Him off a little bit, He'll put a disease on you. Yet the last part of the verse says He is the Lord that heals you. These thoughts contradict each other; the Lord may put sickness on you, but don't worry, because He'll heal you too.

This contradiction should cause a warning sign to light up in our heads. Jesus said in Matthew 12:25, "Every kingdom divided against itself is brought to desolation; and every city or house divided against itself shall not stand" (NKJV). How could the Lord be Jehovah Rapha, "the Lord that healeth thee," and also be "the Lord that maketh thee sick"?

Well, which idea lines up with the nature of God? According to what we looked at earlier, God brings life and not death. Healing is a form of life. Jesus Himself brought healing to the multitudes during His ministry on earth, and according to John 5:19, when Jesus healed people, He was showing us what the Father's actions would be. It says:

> Then Jesus answered and said to them, "Most assuredly, I say to you, the Son can do nothing of Himself, but what He sees the Father do; for whatever He does, the Son also does in like manner (NKJV).

Did Jesus ever put disease on anyone? Did He ever bring misfortune into anyone's life? Never! What did He do? He brought healing, restoration, and deliverance—all of which confirm that the nature of God is to heal, not bring sickness.

How, then, are we supposed to understand Exodus 15:26 and other verses like it that make it seem as though God sometimes puts sickness on people?

Well, it's important to remember that when we speak of the "infallible Word of God," we're referring to the prophets who first spoke God's Word into this earth. Translations are not divinely inspired. Bible scholars bring their own prejudices to their work. The people who translated the Bible into the King James version worked within their own defective understanding of who God is. They saw God as the one who could be responsible for calamity and disease, and as a result, they chose to translate the verse to reflect that.

A while back, I set out to find an answer to this seeming contradiction. When I read the Bible with a concordance (an easy way to find the different possibilities for defining a particular Hebrew word), I found out that this verse could be translated differently than how many translators chose.

Every Hebrew verb can be translated in either a causative or a permissive sense, depending on the idea that's being conveyed. Although verse 26 can be read, "I will put none of these diseases upon thee" when using the causative sense, it can just as accurately be read, "I will permit none of these diseases upon thee."

Can you see the huge difference in each of these interpretations? One says God causes sickness; the other says He permits it. I thoroughly believe the second translation is the more accurate translation, because it lines up with the nature of God as described in the Word. God does permit things to happen in our lives if we're not obedient and responsive to His Word, but He is not the one who brings evil into our lives in any way, shape, or form.

Do you see how the light of the New Testament helps us properly interpret what we see in the Old Testament? As we uncover principles of truth in the Old Testament, they're going to hold true for the whole Bible, but that doesn't mean we interpret the whole Bible on the basis of the Old Testament. We should look at the Old Testament in light of the truths seen in the New Testament; then we'll begin to see how the revelation of the New Testament agrees with the Old Testament rather than how it conflicts with it.

And that's why when we look at Job, we'll look at it in light of the truths seen in the New Testament.

Job in the New Testament

With that in mind, I want to look at the only time Job is mentioned in the New Testament. This will help set our sails for interpreting the rest of Job. James 5:11 says:

Indeed we count them blessed who endure. You have heard of the perseverance of Job and seen the end intended by the Lord—that the Lord is very compassionate and merciful (NKJV).

James didn't remind us of Job's boils, the loss of his children, or the rest of his suffering. James reminds us of Job's patience, his endurance, and something else called "the end of the Lord."

First, that word *patience* doesn't refer to what you think it might. It doesn't mean Job put on a sweet smile of resignation until the torture was over. The dictionary defines patient as "steadfast despite opposition, difficulty, or adversity."[1] The *Strong's Concordance* defines patience as "cheerful endurance" or "constancy."[2] If you combine these definitions, you'll see that patience is being constant and unchanging in the face of external pressure or circumstances.

And ultimately, that's exactly what Job did. Yes, he did waver under pressure and say some wrong things about God, mainly because he was trying to figure out what was happening to him. But Job never turned away from God. He was consistent and unchanging in following Him. And that's what Satan had wanted him to turn from. He was after Job's relationship with God—the very thing Job didn't give him.

Because of that, God was able to bring deliverance to his life. James encourages us to remember and imitate that same type of endurance.

19

The End of the Lord

Also, James tells us to be inspired by something called "the end of the Lord." What was the "end of the Lord" in Job's case? James notes some of it, particularly that the Lord was compassionate and filled with mercy. But we can see the complete end of the story by looking at the end of the book of Job. Job 42 tells us the Lord restored twice as much of everything Job had enjoyed before his trials began. That's what I call a great deliverance!

And as James points out, that is what the book of Job is all about. It's not about *why* the righteous have to suffer. It's not even about *what* the righteous will suffer. It's about a righteous man who clung to his relationship with God, even in the darkest of times. And it's about God's compassion and mercy which will always lead the righteous through to an abundant deliverance.

Taking
Job Apart

Part 2

Job's Limitations

Let's get an image in our minds of who this guy, Job, was.

> *There was a man in the land of Uz, whose name was Job; and that man was blameless and upright, and one who feared God and shunned evil. And seven sons and three daughters were born to him. Also, his possessions were seven thousand sheep, three thousand camels, five hundred yoke of oxen, five hundred female donkeys, and a very large household, so that this man was the greatest of all the people of the East* (Job 1:1–3 NKJV).

Job was a good man; he was "blameless and upright" in the choices he made. (That doesn't mean he was without sin. It means he was complete or mature and lived right before God.) He was a wealthy man with lots of worldly possessions, including a large family. He was "the greatest of all the people of the East."

As you know, all that Job had was taken from him—his family, his possessions, his wealth, and even his health. Before we look at why that happened, let's look at three myths the religious world holds about Job.

Myth 1: Job and His Friends Are Credible Sources of Information.

The first myth we need to debunk is one I've already mentioned. People think Job and his friends were theological experts and that everything they said had merit or was truth.

Nothing could be further from the truth. Since the book of Job is one of the oldest books in the Bible, Job had no scripture to reference when trying to determine who God was. He couldn't turn to the Gospels or the Epistles or anything else. He had no written references in his pursuit of the Lord, although he wished he had:

> *Oh that one would hear me! behold, my desire is, that the Almighty would answer me, and that mine adversary* [referring to God] *had written a book. Surely I would take it upon my shoulder, and bind it as a crown to me* (Job 31:35–36).

Job lived about the same time as Isaac and Jacob. Since he wasn't the seed of Abraham, he wasn't a member of God's family. In other words, he was what Ephesians 2:12 calls an "alien" from the commonwealth of Israel. He had no covenant with God and no promises from God. Moreover, since he was not in a position to receive Jesus as Lord and Savior, he had no indwelling Spirit of God.

Job and his friends did what the rest of us often find ourselves doing. Based on what we know about God (or don't know), we draw conclusions about how He works in our lives. But as we'll continue to find out later, Job and his three friends didn't have a clear revelation of who God is and are mostly wrong in their conclusions.

Job was without a covenant, without promises, without a Bible, and without the Holy Ghost. His information about God was extremely limited. His friends' information about God was just as limited. Because of that, Job and his friends cannot be considered authorities on God or even credible sources of information.

Myth 2: Job's Trials Lasted for Most of His Life.

A second myth we must set aside is that Job's trials lasted a long time. The book of Job seems to continue a long time, and as a result, we're apt to think of it as covering most of Job's life. In actuality, it was only a small portion.

The Bible reports that he lived over two hundred years. Most commentaries agree that his trials only lasted six to nine months.

It's strange how people tend to think of Job as having a hard life. Yes, those six months of trials were extremely difficult (I can't even imagine!), but step back for a moment and put things in perspective. Six to nine months out of two hundred odd years of prosperity and blessing is barely a blip on the radar.

Myth 3: Job Was Poor.

The third myth we need to get rid of is the "poor old Job" cliché that religious tradition has handed down to us. Job was an extremely wealthy man for most of his life (save for those months of his tribulation). Prior to his trials, Job was called "the greatest of all the men of the east"; after his deliverance, he was twice as wealthy as before. And when he did have wealth, he didn't just have a few extra bucks in the bank. To support all his livestock, he had to have a spread of half a million acres. (That's a huge ranch in anybody's terms!) In order to manage all that livestock on that much acreage, he had to have a thousand full-time employees—"a very great household," according to the Bible.

If you translate Job's acreage, livestock, and facilities into today's economic terms, you'd come up with total assets of almost two billion dollars. An undertaking of that size would generate a hundred and fifty million a year in gross revenues. And these are the numbers before calamity happened in his life. After the crisis was over, God gave him twice that much. Job was anything but poor.

The next time somebody says to you, "You're like poor old Job," just smile and say "Thanks!" because that person has blessed you without realizing it.

Ignore the Bad Publicity

Imagine for a moment you got up early one morning, staggered out of bed, and heard the doorbell ring. You've got bed head, or maybe rollers and cold cream. You go to the door in your favorite nightgown, which has a few holes in it. You look terrible. And when you open the door, somebody snaps your picture, says "Thank you," and walks away.

Next morning, you see your picture on the front page of the paper. Everyone who sees your picture in the paper assumes that's who you really are, when it is actually a snapshot of you at your worst.

Religious tradition has done the same thing to Job. They've looked at the book of Job, a snapshot of his life, and said, "This is Job."

But as I've been arguing, it isn't. Besides understanding who God is, we need to understand who Job is. Once we do that, we can better understand why God focuses attention on this particularly difficult time of his life.

5 Job's Calamities

The book of Job can be divided into three segments: destruction, debate, and deliverance. We'll look at each segment, starting with the destruction phase in Job 1:4–5:

> *And his sons would go and feast in their houses, each on his appointed day, and would send and invite their three sisters to eat and drink with them. So it was, when the days of feasting had run their course, that Job would send and sanctify them, and he would rise early in the morning and offer burnt offerings according to the number of them all. For Job said, "It may be that my sons have sinned and cursed God in their hearts." Thus Job did regularly. Now there was a day when the sons of God came to present themselves before the Lord, and Satan also came among them* (NKJV).

Some people are surprised by the last part of this text. They ask, "What's Satan doing in heaven?" Well, the Bible says that in this present dispensation of time, Satan is the prince of the power of the air (Ephesians 2:2). He's not confined to hell (that won't happen until the millennial reign of Christ), so he has freedom to move through the heavens.

We also know from Revelation 12:10 that Satan is the accuser of the brethren. He points out our faults and mistakes. When we pray for God's provision in our lives, Satan points out our inadequacies and claims, "Look! They've blown it. You can't bless them."

Thank God, that's exactly when Jesus, our mediator, stands up and says, "No, I've paid the price for that. They're free to receive the blessing." But when Job was around, that protection wasn't available yet. Job wished that it was:

> *For He is not a man, as I am, that I may answer Him, and that we should go to court together. Nor is there any mediator between us, who may lay his hand on us both. Let Him take His rod away from me, and do not let dread of Him terrify me. Then I would speak and not fear Him, but it is not so with me* (Job 9:32–35 NKJV).

Although he probably didn't realize it, Job was talking about Jesus. Jesus is our mediator between God and man. He is able to bridge the gap of knowledge that Job was keenly aware of. But since Jesus hadn't yet come and died on the cross, humanity didn't have an advocate. Satan had perfectly good grounds for the argument that he leveled against Job in verses 1:7–12:

> *And the Lord said to Satan, "From where do you come?" So Satan answered the Lord and said, "From going to and fro on the earth, and from walking back and forth on it." Then the Lord said to Satan, "Have you considered My servant Job, that there is none like him on the earth, a blameless and upright man, one who fears God and shuns evil?" So Satan answered the Lord and said, "Does Job fear God for nothing? Have You not made a hedge around him, around his household, and around all that he has on every side? You have blessed the work of his hands, and his possessions have increased in the land. But now, stretch out Your hand and touch all that he has, and he will surely curse You to Your face!" And the Lord said to Satan, "Behold, all that he has is in your power; only do not lay a hand on his person." So Satan went out from the presence of the Lord* (NKJV).

Satan was after Job's commitment to the Lord. He wanted Job to curse God. And he tried to make that happen. In the next dozen verses, we see calamity strike.

Bandits raided Job's ranch and killed his servants. A storm blew down his house and killed his children. Verse 20 records Job's response; "Then Job arose, tore his robe, and shaved his head; and he fell to the ground and worshiped" (NKJV).

We could stop our investigation right here and conclude that no matter what calamity may befall you, if you'll do what Job did, making sure that your attitude toward God is right, you'll get through and you'll see the deliverance of the Lord. But I don't think we'd be doing the story of Job justice if we did that. So let's keep reading.

In verse 21, Job spoke the words for which he is most famous: "Naked came I out of my mother's womb, and naked shall I return thither: the Lord gave, and the Lord hath taken away; blessed be the name of the Lord."

How many times have you heard that? "The Lord giveth, and the Lord taketh away; blessed be the name of the Lord." Well-meaning but ignorant Christians have taken this statement and ran with it. They attribute to God everything that happens in their lives, just as Job did. Whole doctrines have been built on this verse. "God may take it away at any moment," they say, "and that's His right because He gave it."

But remember what I pointed out earlier. These words were spoken by a man who had no revelation of God. Plus, he had just gone through horrible calamity in his life. He said what anyone who believes in God but doesn't know Him well might say: "Whatever happens must be of God."

If we keep our beliefs based on the Bible, we'll listen to New Testament truths instead. Yes, like Job, we're to worship when we experience calamity. But we're to understand very clearly that God is not the author of suffering—the enemy is.

Why the Attack?

Why then did God allow Job to be attacked?

Let's back up a bit and look at the conversation between God and Satan (Job 1:8–12). On the surface, this exchange seems to be a wager between God and Satan. God appears to be baiting Satan: "Hey, Satan, see Job down there? Look how good he is. There isn't another one like him." And having tempted Satan, God said, "Go get him," and then made Job accessible so Satan could tear his prosperity to pieces.

That can't be right. God brings life, not death. He is not the author of confusion; He's the author of peace. So what's going on here?

I think the key to understanding this is in verse eight. "And the Lord said unto Satan, Hast thou considered my servant Job?" The King James translation makes it sound as if God is calling Job to Satan's attention, but the literal Hebrew for this expression is, "Hast thou set thy heart on Job?" God wasn't calling Satan's attention to anything. He was simply reading Satan's mind, so to speak, taking note that Satan had already set his heart on Job.

There are people that Satan *can't* attack and there are people he *can* attack. The only people Satan sets his heart on are those he has access to.

> *Be sober, be vigilant; because your adversary the devil walks about like a roaring lion, seeking whom he may devour* (1 Peter 5:8 NKJV).

If Satan could set his heart on just anyone, there would be no point in his "walking to and fro in the earth," right? When Satan told God that he'd been "walking to and fro in the earth," what was he doing? He was "seeking whom he may devour."

God knew this and pointed out what the enemy had already seen. Job had attracted Satan's attention. Satan himself implied as much in verse 10, when he said,

"Hast thou not made an hedge about him, and about his house, and about all that he hath on every side?"

I find it interesting that Satan alluded to a spiritual "hedge" of protection. That lets me know that Satan had run up against such hedges in other people's lives. He knows what a hedge is and he asked God (or possibly taunted Him), "You've got one around Job, haven't you?"

Did Job have a hedge of protection? If he did, why was it down? We're not told exactly. But I'm going to suggest two reasons why Job was open to Satan's attack.

First, it may be as simple as the fact that he had no covenant with God. Everywhere I look in the Bible, supernatural protection is guaranteed only to those who are under the Old or the New Covenant. If our lives are to be redeemed from the curse of the law (the curse that operates in the earth today), we need to be born again, covered by the blood of our Passover Lamb. I don't know of any other guarantee of divine protection.

The text does suggest that Job may have enjoyed limited protection by way of general spiritual law. God said to Satan, "Go ahead, but don't touch his life," implying that Satan had to get permission to attack.

If that's the case, why was permission given?

I believe Job had a problem besides the lack of a covenant: the fear factor. In Job 3:25, Job made a revealing statement: "For the thing which I greatly feared is come upon me, and that which I was afraid of is come unto me." Job's fear, I submit, was the other element that made Satan's attack permissible.

Throughout the Bible, we're told that our lives will reflect our beliefs. What you believe is what you get. This belief is called faith. If you believe the Word of God, it'll produce the blessing of God. If you believe Satan is going to harm you, your fear and worry will produce what you fear the most. The spiritual law is the same in both cases.

What you believe and confess determines what your life becomes, whether for good or for evil.

Ultimately, God didn't bring Job's hedge down. The hedge was already down. Satan had access to Job for one (or both) of two reasons: he had no covenant with God and he was living in fear. All God did was confirm this when He told Satan, in Job 1:12, "Behold, all that he has is in your power."

Whose Responsibility Is It?

God asked Satan the same question in a separate conversation at the beginning of Job chapter 2, and the terminology is the same. After Satan's initial attack on Job, God knew Satan still had his heart set on Job and drew Satan out with the question.

> *Again there was a day when the sons of God came to present themselves before the Lord, and Satan came also among them to present himself before the Lord. And the Lord said to Satan, "From where do you come?" So Satan answered the Lord and said, "From going to and fro on the earth, and from walking back and forth on it." Then the Lord said to Satan, "Have you considered My servant Job, that there is none like him on the earth, a blameless and upright man, one who fears God and shuns evil? And still he holds fast to his integrity, although you incited Me against him, to destroy him without cause"* (Job 2:1–3 NKJV).

Some people get tripped up at the end of this verse. The New King James version reads, "...and still he holds fast to his integrity, although you incited Me against him, to destroy him without cause." People have said to me, "Mac, it says right here that Satan talked God into testing Job, and God brought destruction against him without cause. How can you read it any other way?"

Again, I submit this is a translation error. The Charles Thomson's Septuagint translation provides us with a better understanding of these verses—one that keeps responsibility for Job's problems where it belongs. The last half of verse three reads: "Still he retaineth his innocence, so that thou hast ordered the destruction of his property without accomplishing thy purpose."[1] The responsibility is plainly Satan's, not God's.

God was not behind Job's problems. He didn't use Satan to teach Job a lesson or to punish him. Job lived in fear and he had no covenant with God. Because of these things, he was vulnerable to Satan's attack. And refusing to turn His hand against Job as Satan suggested, the Lord said, "Behold, he's in your hand," a simple statement of fact.

Paul's Thorn

Before we move on, we need to deal specifically with the New Testament text that religious people most often use to confirm the traditional view of Job: the apostle Paul's "thorn."

And lest I should be exalted above measure by the abundance of the revelations, a thorn in the flesh was given to me, a messenger of Satan to buffet me, lest I be exalted above measure. Concerning this thing I pleaded with the Lord three times that it might depart from me. And He said to me, "My grace is sufficient for you, for My strength is made perfect in weakness." Therefore most gladly I will rather boast in my infirmities, that the power of Christ may rest upon me (2 Corinthians 12:7–9 NKJV).

Traditional religion interprets this to say, "God didn't want Paul getting too puffed up with pride because of all the revelation he had, so He turned Satan loose on him. When Paul cried out to God to help him get rid of this thorn in the flesh, God said, 'No, you're just going to have to suffer; I'm not going to help you.' So then Paul said, 'Praise God, I'll glory in my sicknesses and diseases.'"

First of all, if Paul was getting puffed up with pride, Satan wasn't going to do anything to stop it. He loved it. "Pride goes before destruction, and a haughty spirit before a fall" (Proverbs 16:18 NKJV). I guarantee that if pride was the problem, Satan would not have sent messengers to undo it. Paul would have put himself in enough trouble already by being prideful.

Secondly, we've already established the fact that God doesn't inflict sickness and disease on anyone, and He certainly doesn't use Satan to put sickness on someone.

So what exactly are these verses saying?

The "exaltation" Paul was talking about was the lifting up of Jesus. Paul was getting a flood of revelation about the body of Christ; because of that, Jesus was being lifted and exalted through Paul, which is exactly what should happen. The Bible says in 1 Peter 5:6 that if we humble ourselves beneath the mighty hand of God, He will exalt us. Why? Because when people see Jesus in us, they will also see the light of the Gospel and they'll be drawn to Jesus by that light.

Satan saw this happening in Paul's life and decided he'd better do something about it. He sent Paul a messenger who would keep Jesus from being lifted up "above measure" through Paul.

Defining the Thorn

Altogether too many explanations have been made in trying to figure out exactly what this thorn was in Paul's side, so let's go to the Word and let the Bible define itself. (Any time I have a question about a word used in the Bible, I like to use other passages in the Word to define it.) In earlier passages of Scripture, this term *thorn* is never used as a metaphor for sickness or disease, sore eyes, or whatever tradition thinks Paul had. When a thorn is used in the Bible as a figure of speech, it refers to a person or a group of people coming against the children or plan of God.

One example of this is in Numbers 33:55:

> But if you do not drive out the inhabitants of the land from before you, then it shall be that those whom you let remain shall be irritants in your eyes and thorns in your sides, and they shall harass you in the land where you dwell (NKJV).

The Canaanites were called "thorns in your sides" because they were hindering the Jews and limiting the plan of God in their lives. They were doing the same thing that the people persecuting Paul were doing—trying to hinder the light of the Gospel from shining to other people.

From the record we have of Paul's ministry, we know he was beaten, stoned, thrown in jail, persecuted more intensely than just about anyone else in the Bible. Satan moved men to harass him at his meetings, to mock him, to throw rocks at him, to stir up the authorities against him, to get him thrown in jail. And why? So Jesus, in Paul, wouldn't be "exalted above measure."

This persecution was the thorn in Paul's flesh, not a sickness or disease.

The Choice for Deliverance

Now, when Paul cried out to God for deliverance, God did not say, "No, I will not deliver you." God said, "Paul, my grace is sufficient for thee."

God's grace is what saves us (Ephesians 2:8). It not only saves us, but it preserves us, protects us, and delivers us. God simply reminded Paul of this truth: "By My grace, I've already made available the solution to your problem. Use your faith." And the rest of our text shows us how Paul used it.

It's interesting to note that God seemed to be giving Paul a choice about what to do with his "thorn." I think a general biblical principle is presented here. When facing persecution, you can use the strength that comes through God's grace for either endurance or deliverance.

We see this principle in the eleventh chapter of Hebrews, the "Faith Hall of Fame." Wonderful things are listed that various Israelites did by faith. They quenched the violence of fire, escaped the edge of the sword, and so on. But toward the end of the list, it says, "others were tortured, not accepting deliverance; that they might obtain a better resurrection" (verse 35).

Some people chose to suffer. God left it up to them to determine how they wanted to use the power that comes through grace when they faced persecution. I think we have the same choice when faced with persecution. What will give God the greatest visibility: our endurance or our deliverance?

In any case, if we consider everything else the Bible says about the subject, Paul's thorn had nothing to do with "suffering for Jesus" in the way traditional religion imagines it.

Paul's Infirmities

One more point needs to be clarified before we get back to Job. Paul wrote, "Most gladly therefore will I rather glory in my infirmities." Christians are often confused by the word *infirmity*, because in English it usually refers to sickness. But the normal meaning of the Greek word is "weakness" or the frailty of human flesh.[2] Paul is saying, "I'm going to glory in my human frailty that the power of Christ may rest upon me."

Paul had a revelation of what true biblical humility is. He knew he didn't have to be a lowly worm and let the world walk on him. True Christian humility means recognizing that without God we are nothing, but with God we can do all things through Christ who strengthens us.

A Book of Extremes

One last item I want to point out as we wrap up our study of the destruction of Job is that the book of Job is a book of extremes. Job was extremely wealthy, extremely virtuous, and extremely short of information about God. Satan tested him to the extreme in every area of his life. He didn't just have family problems; he lost all his children. He didn't just have financial problems; in today's terms, he lost two billion dollars' worth of assets. He wasn't just sick with the flu; he experienced extreme discomfort in his body.

But the good news is that the glory of his deliverance was extreme.

This is the core message of the book of Job—the deliverance of the Lord. If God brought a glorious deliverance out of Job's troubles and Job didn't have any of the spiritual advantages that we have, how much more will God deliver us from sufferings we may face?

This is the type of understanding we need to have when studying the book of Job.

6 Job's Debate

We've seen the destruction portion of Job; let's take a look at the second section of Job, the debate section. It's fascinating that over 80% of the book of Job is devoted to a conversation between four men who, as I've already stated, didn't know anything about the things of God. Thirty-five chapters are devoted to their various speculations on God and His involvement in the suffering Job was going through.

Why is this important for us to study? Because it shows how people interpret God when they look solely at their circumstances.

Our study of their debate will illuminate some of the wrong perspectives these guys had of God. We won't take the time to thoroughly review all 35 chapters, but we'll pull out important things we can learn from.

God's View of the Debate

Before we do that, let me show you what God had to say about what was spoken during the debate. In chapter 38:2 He says, "Who is this who darkens counsel by words without knowledge?" (NKJV). God said that Job and his friends had been speaking about Him without knowledge. Because of it, God declared, "My wrath is aroused against you and your two friends, for you have not spoken of Me what is right..." (Job 42:7 NKJV).

God was angry and rightfully so. Everything that had been said about Him up to this point offered no truth about who He really is.

Would you like it if an acquaintance of yours told everyone lies about the way you treated your children?

Of course not! You'd be ticked if you knew someone was misrepresenting you, even if they weren't speaking out of malice.

Thankfully, Job responded the right way. He raised his hand and acknowledged his guilt. "Therefore have I uttered that I understood not; things too wonderful for me, which I knew not. ... Wherefore I abhor myself, and repent in dust and ashes" (Job 42:3, 6).

Job knew he'd been speaking wrong things about God and immediately acknowledged it. He saw the truth and repented. And God honored his repentance.

One side note regarding God's response to this debate. At the end of verse 7, God was talking to Job's three friends and said, "My wrath is aroused against you and your two friends, for you have not spoken of Me what is right, *as My servant Job has*" (italics mine).

A minister once said to me that this comment made by God validates everything Job said. I don't agree with his assumption because Job himself repented to God of what he had spoken. When God said, "as my servant Job hath," I believe He's referring to Job's final comment: "I was wrong, and I repent." His repentance was "the thing that is right," not any of his previous statements about God.

God Doesn't Punish Us With Suffering

So let's look at some of the wrong perspectives of God that Job and his friends had. His first friend to speak is Eliphaz the Temanite:

Remember now, who ever perished being innocent? Or where were the upright ever cut off? Even as I have seen, those who plow iniquity and sow trouble reap the same. By the blast of God they perish, and by the breath of His anger they are consumed (Job 4:7–9 NKJV).

The first conclusion an uninformed person will make in trying to understand God through circumstance is that calamity and suffering are God's judgment on sin. Job's two other friends had the same notion and repeated it in chapter after chapter. "Job, you're experiencing these problems because you're sinful. You say you're righteous and you don't know where you missed it, but you're wrong. You've sinned, Job, or you wouldn't be experiencing the judgment of God."

Job's friends were right about one thing. Sin does open us to difficulty. It breaks our fellowship with God and exposes us to the curse that is in the earth. But that doesn't mean God punishes us with sickness or calamity because we've sinned. In John 12:47 Jesus said, "I did not come to judge the world but to save the world" (NKJV).

Disaster is not the fist of God coming down in judgment. It is the hand of God's protection being lifted away. It is absolutely crucial to understand this. God will never judge people by bringing suffering into their lives. His will is always to save us. Only our disobedience can prevent Him from doing so, whether it be deliberate disobedience or merely ignorance like Job's.

Think for a moment about what happened after Adam and Eve sinned. God's hand of protection was lifted allowing evil, pain, and suffering to come into the world. Since then, God has labored to restore His protection to humankind. How does He do that? He does it through obedience. As He told the Israelites in Deuteronomy 28, if you want to be shielded from the pain of the curse, you must obey My Word. If you live according to God's value system (the Bible for us today; the Law for the Israelites in Moses' day), He will see to it that you're blessed and protected. But if you disobey it, He has no choice but to remove His hand of protection, and you'll experience the curse that is in the earth.

Suffering from sin is not God's doing. When we sin, the suffering of the world touches our lives because we've disobeyed God and His protection has been removed.

God Doesn't Use Suffering to Teach Us a Lesson

A second wrong notion about God appears in the next chapter. Eliphaz is still speaking, but his viewpoint is repeated later by Job's other two friends: "Behold, happy is the man whom God corrects; therefore do not despise the chastening of the Almighty. For He bruises, but He binds up; He wounds, but His hands make whole" (Job 5:17–18 NKJV).

I once heard a minister preach that God broke his leg to teach him a lesson. That's the same mentality we see expressed here: God may send calamity, crisis, or suffering to instruct you. He'll make you sore, then bind you up. He'll wound you, then make you whole.

This concept that God uses suffering to teach us a lesson isn't biblical. As we've already seen, God doesn't deal with death. He doesn't deal with confusion, and He will not turn on His children, bringing pain one moment and relief the next. Look at what Jesus said in Matthew 7:11:

If you then, being evil, know how to give good gifts to your children, how much more will your Father who is in heaven give good things to those who ask Him! (NKJV).

Would you teach your son a lesson by taking his hand, putting it on a hot stove, letting his flesh burn a little, and then say, "This is to teach you a lesson. The hot stove burns you. See how it hurts?"

Chances are they'd put you in either the state prison or the state hospital. Yet, we accuse God of doing such things to us—zapping us with calamity, pain, and heartache to teach us lessons. The notion is ridiculous. That is not the way God teaches us.

Along similar lines, I've heard people say, "Well, I know it must have been the will of God that I had that accident, because if I hadn't been lying in the hospital bed, I wouldn't have had the chance to witness to that nurse. I really learned some things then. God spoke to me."

Of course, He did. If you've made a mistake and wound up in the hospital, God will try to correct you. You'd do the same thing if your daughter put her hand on a hot burner. You'd say, "Don't do that again, dear. It hurts."

God does correct us, but He does it through His Word, not through sickness, disease, bankruptcy, or pain. As Paul wrote 2 Timothy 3:16–17:

All scripture is given by inspiration of God, and is profitable for doctrine, for reproof, for correction, for instruction in righteousness: that the man of God may be perfect, thoroughly furnished unto all good works.

God doesn't deliberately harm us so we'll learn how to be a better person. If you've been taught that sort of religious trash, get rid of it. It will rob you of a scriptural view of who God is and the kind of treatment you can expect from Him. He instructs and corrects His people through the Word, not through pain and suffering.

The Worm Syndrome

There's one more misconception about God that I want to show you in chapter 25. Job's friend, Bildad the Shuhite, makes this comment:

How then can man be righteous before God? Or how can he be pure who is born of a woman? If even the moon does not shine, and the stars are not pure in His sight, how much less man, who is a maggot, and a son of man, who is a worm?" (Job 25:4–6 NKJV).

This text has been misused through countless generations to poison the body of Christ. The "worm syndrome," as I've often called it, says you're just a worm and deserve to be squashed by your circumstances. Man is such a low creature he merits nothing better than a life of calamity and suffering. "I'm not worthy! My righteousness is as filthy rags." You'd never believe how much of the Church is in bondage to this mentality. And it's completely wrong.

God sees you differently. He made you in His image and likeness. He created you to have dominion over this earth and everything in it. He endured the agony of the Cross so you could become a member of His eternal family, taking on His very own nature and sharing in all the blessings of heaven. That's the born again you. You are not a worm.

Satan would gladly have us walking around with our head hung low, wallowing in the suffering we think God inflicted; when, in reality, we should be running around, heads held high, rejoicing in the fact that God will deliver us from whatever circumstances we face. With God on our side, who can be against us?

Don't allow the misconceptions of Job's friends to influence your opinion of who God is. Keep your foundation solid and learn from their mistakes. Paint a biblical picture of who God is and never let that go, no matter what circumstances come your way.

7 The "Wisdom" of Job

How many times have you heard someone say, "We never really know what to expect from God, because He is sovereign and can do what He wants. Sometimes the Lord brings good, and sometimes He brings evil"?

Usually this type of statement comes from someone who is quoting Job. Job made multiple statements along these lines, including:

"'Naked I came from my mother's womb, and naked shall I return there. The Lord gave, and the Lord has taken away; blessed be the name of the Lord" (Job 1:21 NKJV).

"Shall we indeed accept good from God, and shall we not accept adversity?" (Job 2:10 NKJV).

"For the arrows of the Almighty are within me; my spirit drinks in their poison; the terrors of God are arrayed against me" (Job 6:4 NKJV).

I cringe every time I hear statements along these lines because it's counter to the truth we see in the New Testament. As I've already shown you, the Lord does not give both life and death. His only gift to us is life and life more abundantly.

James 1:17 says, "Every good gift and every perfect gift is from above, and comes down from the Father of lights, with whom there is no variation or shadow of turning" (NKJV). Jeremiah 29:11 says, "For I know the thoughts that I think toward you, says the Lord, thoughts of peace and not of evil, to give you a future and a hope" (NKJV).

God is unchanging in His nature and does not inflict evil on anyone. James 1:13 even tells us that it's not possible for God to test us with evil:

Let no one say when he is tempted, "I am tempted by God"; for God cannot be tempted by evil, nor does He Himself tempt anyone (NKJV).

That word *tempted* literally means "to test" or "try."[1] God doesn't use evil to tempt, test, or try anyone—including Job. No matter the reason your natural mind can conjure up, attributing evil to God is a dangerous path to walk on. We should never go there. God *never* tempts anyone with evil.

If you don't know the Word, it's far too easy to fall into the same trap that Job fell into and think God is behind your problems. *God is sovereign. He could stop this thing if He wanted to. Therefore, it must be His will that it is happening.*

But what Job was said was wrong, and ultimately, he had to repent of what he said. If you share his point of view, change it. God is not behind the trouble you face. Whatever catastrophe you are dealing with, God did not bring it into your life.

Take an Attitude Check

In addition to a wrong perspective of God, Job also had an attitude problem. "Therefore I will not restrain my mouth; I will speak in the anguish of my spirit; I will complain in the bitterness of my soul" (Job 7:11 NKJV).

A lot of Christians use this verse as an excuse for saying whatever they want about the circumstances they face. One time, after I'd preached on confessing the Word rather than negative circumstances, someone referred me to this verse. She said, "We need to be truthful and say whatever is happening, just as Job did."

Job did speak the natural truth about his circumstances, but do we have any indication that helped him?

No. On the contrary, I believe his words only prolonged the suffering he was going through.

If you want to perpetuate trouble and difficulty, then by all means talk about your anguish, complain, and say whatever you want to say. You'll continue to suffer as Job did.

Don't Grow Bitter

In Job 9:18, Job spoke again of his troubles: "He will not allow me to catch my breath, but fills me with bitterness" (NKJV). We all know Christians who are bitter about their lives. As a pastor, I probably run into them more often than you do. Churches are filled with people who are bitter about hurtful things that happened when they were children—abusive situations, divorces, physical problems, accidents, financial crises. Some Christians grow bitter about life or even God, especially when they compare themselves to others who seem to be more blessed. It's as if they have good reason to be bitter because God failed to do what they thought was best or because He allowed this or that to happen.

But there's a terrible danger in this response to life's insults. If we don't deal with the bitterness in our lives, our difficulties will be perpetuated just as Job's were. If we allow our hearts to be filled with it and do nothing about it, we'll continue to suffer difficulty and calamity.

Get rid of your bitterness. Don't extend your circumstances by speaking out of the frustrations you feel. God has no desire to make you bitter, and He's done nothing for you to be bitter about. He's given you all that's necessary to purge bitterness from your life and replace it with the faith that brings godly results.

A Wrong View of Predestination

Christians have also picked up on the idea Job presents in chapter 23:14. "For He performs what is appointed for me, and many such things are with Him" (NKJV).

The modern version of this verse is: "Whatever happens to me, whether good or bad, is God's predestined plan for my life." People back this verse up by quoting Ephesians 1:4–5:

Just as He chose us in Him before the foundation of the world, that we should be holy and without blame before Him in love, having predestined us to adoption as sons by Jesus Christ to Himself, according to the good pleasure of His will (NKJV).

People conclude that these verses indicate God predestined us to be members of His family before the foundation of the world. But Scripture does not suggest that God's plan for your life will unfold no matter what choices you make. Predestination should be understood within the framework of our free moral agency. Our choices matter. God created us to be free moral agents.

God has a plan for you that is more wonderful than you can imagine. First Corinthians 2:9 says that eye hasn't seen, ear hasn't heard, and the heart of man can't know how wonderful are the things that God has prepared for those who love Him. God has a destiny for you that will knock your socks off. But you have to choose that path. You have to be a seeker of God to understand His destiny for you. Then you have to make choices that take you in the right direction. This is why God says, "I have set before you life and death, blessing and cursing; therefore choose life, that both you and your descendants may live" (Deuteronomy 30:19 NKJV).

The choice is yours. God's got a plan for you, but you must make choices that will put it into effect.

Death Isn't From God

We need to consider one more mistake of Job's before we move on. Job said, "For I know that You will bring me to death, and to the house appointed for all living" (Job 30:23 NKJV).

Some people read this verse the same way they read Job 1:21—that God is in the death business. They think that someone may experience premature death or the things that lead to death if God wants to glorify Himself in that manner, or if He needs to preserve you from some horrible circumstance down the road of life, or if He wants your companionship so badly that He just can't resist "taking you home."

Death has never been God's idea. He didn't bring death onto the scene; death entered the world through Adam's sin (Romans 5:12). Ever since the Fall, God has labored to get rid of it. So far, He's removed the sting of death through the victory of Jesus' death and resurrection (1 Corinthians 15:55), and ultimately, physical death will be put under foot in the next dispensation.

Until then, because of the Fall, "it is appointed unto men once to die" (Hebrews 9:27). Now that doesn't mean God is going to remove people whenever He pleases. The Bible says we can have long life—at least 70 or 80 years. (Look at Psalm 90:10 and 91:16.) I don't know about you, but if the Lord tarries, I'm planning on staying around a long, long time!

We can live a long and prosperous life; in fact, that's what God wants us to do. Premature death isn't His idea. And that's why Job's observations shouldn't alter your view of God. God is in the life-giving business, not the death business.

Don't let Job's incorrect assumptions alter your view of God. Be assured of this truth: God's will for you is life, not death; blessing, not cursing.

Don't Blame God

Do you see the general theme that's coming through each wrong perspective of God we see? People all too easily blame God for the suffering they go through. They seem to be continually attracted to the idea that Job and his friends had: whatever happens is the will of God, and there's nothing you can do about it.

I've always wondered why people fight for their right to suffer and then blame God for it. Then I realized it's the easy way to go. When you buy into this notion, it takes the responsibility for your life off you and puts it on a sovereign God. Ultimately, it makes it easy for you to be spiritually lazy and complacent, which is a dangerous place to be. That's why it's vital to recognize these wrong perceptions of God, alter them, and take responsibility for the path God wants you to walk out in your life.

Turning Job Around

Before we turn to the deliverance portion of the book of Job, we need to spend a moment with the young man named Elihu. He's the person who held his peace until Job's three friends were finished and then spoke for six chapters.

Christian views of Elihu's contribution vary greatly. Some Bible students think he was a brash youngster who said nothing worth our attention. Others suggest he was a spokesman for the Almighty, that everything he said was true, and that he's the only one of the bunch who represented God correctly.

The truth probably lies somewhere between these extremes. In light of what we've learned about God's nature, we can find misstatements that Elihu made. Just like Job's other friends, he had limited information and can't be considered an authority on the nature of God. But he's the only one of Job's four advisers whom God did not rebuke, and that is certainly worth noticing.

I think the reason he wasn't rebuked was because Elihu steered Job away from his circumstances and pointed him to the one thing that could have revealed God to him—God's enduring works of creation. Look at what he said in Job 37:14–16:

Listen to this, O Job; stand still and consider the wondrous works of God. Do you know when God dispatches them, and causes the light of His cloud to shine? Do you know how the clouds are balanced, those wondrous works of Him who is perfect in knowledge? (NKJV).

Elihu recognized the intricacies of creation. He knew that when you look at creation, you see divine order and the absence of confusion and chaos. And when you see that, you can know that God couldn't ordain calamity.

He concluded in verse 23: "As for the Almighty, we cannot find Him; He is excellent in power, in judgment and abundant justice; He does not oppress" (NKJV).

Elihu was exactly right. Creation shows us who God is. Even today, we can look at creation and see God. Go out into the woods, stand on the edge of a lake, and watch a sunrise. Anyone who can do that and say there's no God or that God is the author of confusion is simply dead. God shouts His majesty, His love, His order, His power to us through His creation.

In a sense, God endorsed Elihu's comments because God seemed to pick up where Elihu left off. When God spoke in chapter 38, He kept talking about creation:

Where were you when I laid the foundations of the earth? Tell Me, if you have understanding. Who deter-mined its measurements? Surely you know! Or who stretched the line upon it? To what were its foundations fastened? Or who laid its cornerstone, when the morning stars sang together, and all the sons of God shouted for joy? (Job 38:4–7 NKJV).

Elihu wasn't perfect, but he definitely did some-thing right, and that's something we should pay attention to.

Warning of Wrong Perspectives

The next time you read through the debate chap-ters in Job, read them carefully. If you find your opinions mirrored in the opinions of Job and his friends, repent. Mistaken notions about God will produce trouble for you, and they'll sustain your experience of that trouble, just as they did Job's.

Countless Christians unconsciously do what Job and his friends did. They let their views of God be shaped by their own experiences of suffering. And this is why I believe the book of Job was given to us. It warns of the skewed views that can so easily become a part of your perception of God if you aren't careful.

Even when God doesn't seem to answer your prayers right away or things work out differently than you thought they would, you must be absolutely deliberate in keeping your views of God based on the Bible, not on circumstances. Look at the truths of God's nature found in the New Testament. See how Jesus defined Himself and the Father. Those truths should be the basis for our understanding of who God is.

When you have a skewed view of God and see Him as the author of or somehow connected to your suffering, you'll find yourself enduring the pain far longer than needed because you don't know where the suffering came from.

You'll find plenty of verses in the book of Job that may sound true, even noble, but as I mentioned earlier, everything said by Job and his friends was grounded in misconceptions that made God furious: "You've kindled my wrath against you."

I don't want that and neither do you.

Putting
Job Back
Together

Part 3

9 Steps Toward Deliverance

We've walked through the destruction and debate portion of Job, so now let's look at the most exciting part of the book—the deliverance part.

Job positioned himself to experience a spectacular deliverance of God with almost no spiritual resources. How? There were five things he did that aligned his life and his attitude with God's best for his life. If we can learn from these steps and apply them to our own lives regardless of what we're suffering, we can experience a glorious "end of the Lord" just as Job did.

Step #1: An Unwavering Commitment to the Lord

The first step Job made toward deliverance is seen in Job 13:15. He made a remarkable comment: "Though he slay me, yet will I trust in him."

Commitment. Even though Job thought God was behind his trouble, he still said, "Yet will I trust in Him."

We need to have that same attitude. Commitment has to be in place before deliverance can ever be ours. No matter what's happening to us and even when we don't understand it, when we're determined not to turn our backs on Him, we'll experience the Lord's delivering power.

Commitment to God starts with commitment to His Word, because God and His Word are one (John 1:1). Commitment to His Word means you are committed to believing and obeying His commandments. That's how you keep the door open for God's power to work in your life.

Let me show you what I mean. Say you've been tithing for a year or two and you haven't seen your finances increase. What should you do next? Should you stop tithing because you haven't seen results? No, you should remain committed to God's Word. Keep tithing whether or not you've seen the manifestation of His promises.

What if you've had hands laid on you for healing but you haven't yet seen the manifestation of your healing? Do you stop believing? No, you remain committed to believing what His Word says—that you are healed by Jesus' stripes (1 Peter 2:24) and the prayer of faith will heal the sick (James 5:15).

Many people haven't arrived at this level of commitment yet. People "try" the Word on for size. They give it a shot for a few months. As long as matters work out to their satisfaction, they'll stick with it. But if situations run counter to their prayers and six months pass without seeing God's answer and nothing's changed, they'll say, "So long. This deal doesn't work. I'm going back to my own way of doing it."

If you want God to move on your behalf, you'll have to be just as committed as Job was. You'll have to commit to follow the Lord and His Word regardless of your limited human understanding. (If you could intellectually embrace everything that happened, God wouldn't be much of a God, would He?) The Word does not and will not change no matter what circumstance you are facing. It remains true, even when things aren't lining up like you thought they would.

An unshakeable, unswerving commitment to God—that's the first step toward seeing the deliverance of the Lord in your life.

Step #2: Avoiding Hearsay

The second step toward deliverance is found in Job 42:5: "I have heard of You by the hearing of the ear, but now my eye sees You" (NKJV).

Up until this point, Job had only heard about God through the "hearing of the ear," which refers to hearing people speak about God naturally. He's not referring to the spiritual hearing we see in Romans 10:17 ("Faith comes by hearing, and hearing by the word of God").

When you hear the Word preached, those words carry anointing and bring faith, quite the opposite of the hearsay you hear from other people.

Job makes a necessary move away from what he's heard others say about God to a personal revelation of who God really is.

His revelation of God wasn't seen through natural eyes. Job began to see God through the spiritual eyes of his understanding, which Paul prayed in Ephesians 1:18: "...the eyes of your understanding being enlightened." Job saw for himself who God was. He had a personal revelation of God.

Just like Job, you need to move away from hearsay. From my experience, hearsay is involved in every warped view of God; and most often, it's at the root of each problem. "Well, you know, I heard from my good friend, who's a wonderful Christian, that he believed and stood in faith for months and months, and healing didn't come. So it must be the will of God that some people are sick."

We have no excuse to be dependent on hearsay. We have the Word of God, the ministry of the Holy Spirit, and creation. If you've never invited the Holy Spirit to reveal the truth of God's Word to your heart and to reveal the character of God to you, I encourage you to do it right away. Getting a revelation for yourself of who God really is requires you to close your ears to hearsay.

Step #3: Repentance

After receiving a clear, personal revelation of God, Job took his third step toward deliverance: "Wherefore I abhor myself, and repent in dust and ashes" (Job 42:6). Job repented.

Repentance doesn't just simply mean we are sorry. It means we are purposely changing the direction of our lives. Usually, it means turning away from sin we've committed.

It's interesting to note the Bible says in all his trials, Job didn't sin. If that's the case, what was he repenting of? Words. Job said to God, "I have uttered what I did not understand" (Job 42:3 NKJV), and then he repented of those utterances.

Remember what Job said in Job 7:11? "Therefore I will not restrain my mouth; I will speak in the anguish of my spirit; I will complain in the bitterness of my soul" (NKJV). Job didn't watch what he said. He spoke what he thought without realizing the meaning behind it.

Too many Christians do the same thing. They fail to connect with the power of God and see His grace manifest in their lives because they say whatever they want to say. They don't "refrain their mouths." If they want deliverance, though, they'll have to come to the same conclusion Job did: repent, not just of wrong behavior but also of wrong words.

Proverbs 18:21 says, "Death and life are in the power of the tongue." Jesus said by your words, you'll be justified or condemned (Matthew 12:37). You can't speak words of death and corruption and expect to enter into the restoring grace of God. You're going to have to deal with wrong words: harsh words you spoke to your spouse; words of unbelief ("I don't know how we can pay these bills"); words of complaint ("I don't know why this is happening, I've been tithing for a year").

Repent by saying, "God, I blew it, and I'm going to change the way I speak." Then begin speaking words of life, words that line up with the Word of God, words that come to you from the Word of God by the Spirit of God.

So far, we've learned the road to deliverance starts with a commitment to God and His Word and is followed by receiving our own revelation of God instead of living by hearsay. The third step is changing the words that we speak.

Step #4: Forgive and Forget

Job's fourth step on his road to deliverance is found in Job 42:10: "And the Lord turned the captivity of Job, when he prayed for his friends."

Being that prayer is your personal communion with God, it will always be essential to your deliverance. Too many people want to go to a deliverance service on Friday night and have someone else pray for them, casting out of them whatever they need deliverance from.

That sort of prayer has its place, but it's not the route to deliverance in the broader sense we've been discussing. We have to establish personal communion with God before we can expect His power to flow in our lives. Job's captivity was turned when he prayed.

Part of the reason why God directed Job to pray for his friends was because Job had to deal with the unforgiveness stored up in his heart. As Jesus said in Mark 11:25, "And whenever you stand praying, if you have anything against anyone, forgive him, that your Father in heaven may also forgive you your trespasses" (NKJV).

Unforgiveness cannot remain in our lives. And Job had a lot of opportunity to hold an offense against his friends. If you review the debate (chapters 4 through 30), you'll see the four men said some tough things to one another, resulting in a build up of poison, hurt, and bitterness.

In commanding Job to pray for his friends, I believe God was saying, "Job, before deliverance can come to you, you're going to have to deal with unforgiveness." The same is true for us. We can't pray effectively unless we forgive, and God can't forgive us and answer our prayers until we do.

Now it's easy to say "I forgive you." It's a different story when you realize that biblical forgiveness is defined as forgetting. You haven't forgiven if you haven't forgotten. Too often in counseling situations I see people who'll say, "Oh, I've forgiven them." But then for the next hour, they'll recount in great depth and detail all the pain the other person had inflicted on them. Then they wonder why the power of God is so conspicuously absent from their lives.

Forgiveness hasn't happened if we haven't forgotten.

When God looks at people, He doesn't see all that's wrong with them. He sees them as people He loves so much that He sent Jesus to die for them. We should see people the same way.

We have to quit seeing people on the basis of how they've wronged us, no matter how vile it may have been. When we see people from God's point of view, we won't dwell on the unjust things they've done to us. Instead, we'll be able to pray for them out of a true heart of forgiveness.

This is what God is telling Job in chapter 42: "Job, you need to pray for your friends, because there's unforgiveness there and it'll stand between you and deliverance."

Forgiveness is the fourth step to deliverance. We have to forgive, and then we have to forget.

Step #5: Serving Others

The fifth step toward deliverance can also be seen in verse ten: Job prayed for his friends. He took his eyes off everything that was wrong in his life and focused his attention on somebody else's need.

This is the final key to your deliverance. You've got to get your eyes off everything you need and begin concerning yourself with the needs of others. This is a hard lesson for our flesh to learn, but it's an absolutely essential one. We have to get rid of the self-absorption that says, "My problem is worse than what anyone else is going through."

Most people, Christians included, spend their whole lives addressing their own problems. They never get the revelation that the greatest source of happiness available to them is to help others with their problems. Until I realized this, I was one miserable human being. It's a lesson that too many of us never learn, and we miss out on the Lord's deliverance as a result.

Let's look again at God's words to Eliphaz the Temanite:

> *Now therefore, take for yourselves seven bulls and seven rams, go to My servant Job, and offer up for yourselves a burnt offering; and My servant Job shall pray for you. For I will accept him, lest I deal with you according to your folly; because you have not spoken of Me what is right, as My servant Job has." ... And the Lord restored Job's losses when he prayed for his friends* (Job 42:8, 10 NKJV).

Job's three friends had set themselves up to experience what Job was going through, and God wanted to help them out. Galatians 6:1 can help us better understand this: "Brethren, if a man is overtaken in any trespass, you who are spiritual restore such a one in a spirit of gentleness, considering yourself lest you also be tempted" (NKJV).

When you correct fellow Christians whose sins or errors of judgment have laid them open to Satan's attacks, you must do it meekly or you'll expose yourself to whatever is threatening them. In keeping with this New Testament text, God was saying to Job, "Your three friends are in a dangerous place. I don't want them to have to go through what you've been through. I want you to pray for them. They're not in a position to approach Me right now, but when they make proper sacrifice, I'll receive your prayer. I want you to minister to their needs. You can help them ward off calamity."

Remember, these are men with whom Job has just been in a shouting match. He's still hurting, too; he hasn't received deliverance yet. But in the midst of Job's pain, God said, "Job, I want to use you to help your friends." And Job must come to the place where he can be used by God before God will be able to meet his need.

The story ends well: Job took the last step that all of us must take in order to experience deliverance. He began to serve the needs of others. This phrase sums up everything we're called to do and to be as Christians on this earth. We're here to serve the needs of other people; and when we do so, we open ourselves up to the delivering power of God.

A major reason why the enemy brings trials into your life is to distract you from God's primary call: to serve. If Satan can get you concerned exclusively with poor ol' me, what you need, your own agenda, your program, he can prevent you both from serving others and from experiencing deliverance.

The whole New Testament brings home this truth. Philippians 2:4–9 is a good example:

Let each of you look out not only for his own interests, but also for the interests of others. Let this mind be in you which was also in Christ Jesus, who, being in the form of God, did not consider it robbery to be equal with God, but made Himself of no reputation, taking the form of a bond-servant, and coming in the likeness of men. And being found in appearance as a man, He humbled Himself and became obedient to the point of death, even the death of the cross. Therefore God also has highly exalted Him and given Him the name which is above every name (NKJV).

Here as elsewhere, we're told to be conformed to the image of Jesus. How do we do that? We do it by becoming a servant. When we do, we open ourselves to the delivering power of God.

God's Definition of Service

When you think of serving others, don't think about it narrowly. Understand how God defines service. He doesn't just mean baking a cake and running it over to your neighbor or helping clean someone's house. That could be what you're called to do from time to time, but only one kind of service will make a lasting difference in people's lives; and that's getting Jesus to them—getting the unbeliever saved and getting the Christian grown up in the Word of God.

This is exactly what Jesus Himself did. He helped people out in common ways—feeding them loaves and fishes, turning water into wine, cooking breakfast for the disciples after His resurrection—but His primary concern was to minister salvation to them by the Word of God.

You can do the same thing. Help other people get connected with God in any way you can, just as Job did when he acted as an intercessor for his friends.

What's the best way to do it? There are all sorts of ways you can do it. Invite a friend to church. Give someone a tract. Buy your neighbor a book. Send a friend a teaching CD. Share your testimony. Call your friend and invite him or her to church again.

This is the best way you can serve other people. When you see someone else in need, serve that person, especially with the Word of God, no matter how great your own need may be or how loudly your flesh is demanding your attention. You'll open the door to your own deliverance.

I'll talk about this fundamental principle further in later chapters. For the moment, let's summarize the five steps to deliverance we've seen in the example of Job. If they worked for him, they will surely work for us.

- Have an unshakeable commitment to God and His Word.
- Receive an authentic revelation of God, not based on hearsay.
- Repent of wrong words in addition to wrong behavior.
- Forgive those who have offended us and forget the offenses.
- Turn our attention and efforts to serving others.

What can we expect will happen when we do these things? Job 42:10–17 shows us Job's glorious deliverance. The Lord turned his captivity, gave him twice as much as he had before, blessed him with fourteen thousand sheep, six thousand camels, a thousand yoke of oxen, a thousand she asses, and a whole new family—seven beautiful sons and three daughters.

Now that's a glorious end of the Lord!

Let the New Testament stand your traditional view of Job on its head. As you interpret Job in light of the Gospel, you'll see glorious truth that will set you on your own path to deliverance.

Redefining Suffering

Part 4

Do Christians Have to Suffer at All?

If Christians are not supposed to suffer as Job did, do we have to suffer at all?

Yes. We see this presented in 1 Peter 5:10: "But the God of all grace, who hath called us unto his eternal glory by Christ Jesus, after that ye have suffered a while, make you perfect, stablish, strengthen, settle you."

What suffering is he talking about? Look at Hebrews 5:8–9:

> *Though he were a Son, yet learned he obedience by the things which he suffered; and being made perfect, he became the author of eternal salvation unto all them that obey him.*

Jesus suffered. Through that suffering, He learned obedience and became perfect (or you could say mature). Since He provides our pattern of life here on earth, we can know that there is something we have to suffer too; something that will bring us to a place of maturity where we lay hold on the eternal salvation that is available to us, just as Jesus did.

What kind of suffering did Jesus go through? That's what I want to show you in the next few chapters.

Jesus Wasn't Poor

First, we need to address one religious mindset that people often have about the suffering of Jesus. They jump up and say, "Well, Jesus suffered because He was poor, so we'll need to suffer like that." They use Matthew 8:20 to back up their theory:

And Jesus said to him, "Foxes have holes and birds of the air have nests, but the Son of Man has nowhere to lay His head" (NKJV).

Contrary to what some think, this verse isn't a reference to how poor Jesus was. It simply is a reference to Jesus' traveling ministry. He traveled light; because of the call of God on His life, He had no place to lay His head. His ministry would have been different if He'd had a house and a wife and kids.

I'm ready to argue that Jesus had a prosperous, flourishing ministry. Think about these facts for a moment.

Seventy-some disciples followed Him everywhere He went. The ministry had enough income to support all those disciples and their families.

The ministry had enough income to require a treasurer. How many of us are at the point where we need a Judas to keep track of our finances and a big bag to carry our funds around in?

The treasury bag was big enough that Judas could steal from it without getting caught. If there'd been only a few coins in the bottom, Peter would have noticed and crushed Judas as soon as he started dipping. Judas would have been history, right there.

Jesus had the resources of heaven at His disposal. How many of us have given a seated dinner to 15,000 people, feeding them all loaves and fishes with plenty of leftovers?

How many of us go fishing when it's time to pay our taxes?

Don't tell me Jesus was poor. He had all sufficiency in all things. The Bible says that we, too, have all sufficiency in all things (2 Corinthians 9:8). The idea that we have to suffer through poverty because Jesus was poor is completely wrong.

The Suffering of Jesus

If Jesus didn't have to suffer financially, what did He have to suffer? Well, before Jesus could work one miracle, deliver one oppressed person, or do anything else to change this world, He had to be tempted. And this is the first kind of suffering we see Jesus dealing with.

Then Jesus was led up by the Spirit into the wilderness to be tempted by the devil. And when He had fasted forty days and forty nights, afterward He was hungry. Now when the tempter came to Him, he said, "If You are the Son of God, command that these stones become bread." But He answered and said, "It is written, 'Man shall not live by bread alone, but by every word that proceeds from the mouth of God.'" Then the devil took Him up into the holy city, set Him on the pinnacle of the temple, and said to Him, "If You are the Son of God, throw Yourself down. For it is written: 'He shall give His angels charge concerning you,' and, 'In their hands they shall bear you up, lest you dash your foot against a stone.'" Jesus said to him, "It is written again, 'You shall not tempt the Lord your God.'" Again, the devil took Him up on an exceedingly high mountain, and showed Him all the kingdoms of the world and their glory. And he said to Him, "All these things I will give You if You will fall down and worship me." Then Jesus said to him, "Away with you, Satan! For it is written, 'You shall worship the Lord your God, and Him only you shall serve.'" Then the devil left Him, and behold, angels came and ministered to Him (Matthew 4:1–11 NKJV).

Jesus had to get His flesh under control before He could be useful to God. So do we. But I guarantee your flesh will not like it. It's painful when you tell your body, "No." This is why I consider resisting temptation a type of suffering. It's probably the lowest level that we'll experience. Sometimes it produces discomfort for your flesh, sometimes torment. But the flesh cannot master us. We have to master its desires. Until we do, God won't move us to the next level of His plan for us.

It's important to notice that Jesus took Satan seriously. So should we. Too many Christians think of Satan as a cartoon character or a leftover from Halloween. But that's a huge mistake. If you're going to deal properly with Satan and his influence on your flesh, you'll have to know that he is just as real as God. The same Bible that tells us about Jesus tells us about Satan. Until you accept this, you'll never be able to get the upper hand over your enemy, and he'll be free to block the flow of blessings in your life.

Resisting Your Flesh

What does resisting temptation involve? We can distinguish three different kinds of resistance in the account of Jesus' temptation. The first is the simplest. It has to do with the denial of our flesh's cravings when they get in the way of God's plan.

Now when the tempter came to Him, he said, "If You are the Son of God, command that these stones become bread." But He answered and said, "It is written, 'Man shall not live by bread alone, but by every word that proceeds from the mouth of God'" (Matthew 4:3–4 NKJV).

Jesus had been fasting for forty days and nights. At this point, He was hungry. He could have easily turned those stones to bread and made Himself supper, but He instead chose to ignore Satan's temptation and deny the cravings of His flesh.

Obviously, Satan will not come and taunt you directly as he did Jesus. It's more subtle in our lives. Your flesh may clamor for popularity, fame, power, or success in business. It may demand temptations such as sex, food, tobacco, or liquor.

Often, the flesh wants something that is in complete opposition to what God wants. Other times, it wants something that is innocent in itself. Whatever it is, if the flesh wants something that diverts you from God's plan for your life or causes you to sin, you need to resist the temptation to partake in it.

Don't Tempt God

The second kind of satanic lure we see in Matthew chapter 4 is the temptation to tempt God:

And said to Him, "If You are the Son of God, throw Yourself down. For it is written: 'He shall give His angels charge concerning you,' and, 'In their hands they shall bear you up, lest you dash your foot against a stone.'" Jesus said to him, "It is written again, 'You shall not tempt the Lord your God'" (Matthew 4:6–7 NKJV).

Just as he did to Jesus, Satan's going to come to you and say, "If you're a child of God, you should be able to do anything at all and God will see that it turns out right."

Christians may test God by saying, "Okay, let's see if healing is for real; I'll go up to the altar and get hands laid on me and see if it works." Or "I'm going to tithe for a few months; if it doesn't work, I'll go back to the way I was doing it before."

But that isn't faith; that's testing God. It won't bring a response from Him, and the people who do it won't mature as Christians. God doesn't respond to our little tests. He responds to faith. If we want to grow in Him and receive His blessings, we're going to have to resist the temptation to test Him.

Put God First

The third of Satan's appeals to our flesh is the temptation to worship other gods.

Again, the devil took Him up on an exceedingly high mountain, and showed Him all the kingdoms of the world and their glory. And he said to Him, "All these things I will give You if You will fall down and worship me." Then Jesus said to him, "Away with you, Satan! For it is written, 'You shall worship the Lord your God, and Him only you shall serve'" (Matthew 4:8–10 NKJV).

It's easy to say, "Lord, you are my God. I worship you alone." It is much harder to make that a reality. All of us have the tendency to think we've made God to be number one in our lives, when the truth of the matter is that we've allowed other priorities to sneak ahead of the Lord. But let me tell you, God isn't about to take second place to anybody's priority.

You need to be ruthlessly honest with yourself about this matter. Ask yourself if God is first place in your life or is there something else that has taken priority above Him?

False gods often lay a subtle claim to your worship. Sometimes your business can become a false God to you. For others, it's their profession or trying to achieve an advanced education. For others, it might be their retirement plans. I've even seen families who worship their kids and allow everything, including God, to revolve around their children.

I'm not suggesting that college degrees, business success, and a loving family aren't good things. They are good—but they must not take priority over God in your life. God says He'll have no other gods before Him. That means we must make Him to be our number-one priority.

Of course, your flesh isn't going to go easily in that direction. It's going to put up a fight to keep what it wants as priority in your life.

A lot of people purposely avoid putting God first place in their lives because they know their flesh is going to fuss. They are going to have to suffer some discomfort in order to keep God as their number-one priority. But if we fail to deal with our flesh, we'll never mature in Christ.

Resist With the Spirit's Strength

Through all this talk about temptation, we need to remember that we don't have to resist our flesh in our own strength. We can use the strength that God supplies. The truth is, without the Spirit, you won't have the ability to quit the alcohol or the dope, the gossip or the backbiting, or whatever it is you haven't gotten a handle on. The Holy Spirit is the one who empowers you to get rid of these things if you make it possible for Him to move on your behalf.

Besides, the Spirit was the one who led Jesus into the wilderness for a showdown with Satan. God doesn't want you to step aside for Satan. He wants you to walk on his face. It's easier to say, "God, take me around these temptations" and be insulated from the unpleasantness. But in reality, when temptation rears its ugly head, the Spirit won't take you around it, He'll take you through it!

How do you rely on the Spirit's strength? You do it by denying your flesh.

This is what we see Jesus doing in the wilderness. He fasted forty days and nights denying His flesh. Although the Lord isn't asking us to imitate that exact fast, the principle of fasting or denying the flesh is the same for whatever appetite you need to get rid of.

People often come to me saying, "Pray for me that I won't want alcohol any more" or "...that I won't crave cigarettes any more" or "...that I'll be delivered from pornography." But that's not how it works. We're free moral agents; the decision has to be yours. Quit asking God to take cigarettes away from you. Quit praying that He'll deliver you from booze or gossip or lust or whatever you're struggling with. You have to make the decision; put your foot down and say, "That's it! I'm not going to be ruled by this body of flesh any longer."

However, that won't be the last thing you have to do. Satan will do the same thing to you that he did to Jesus in the wilderness. He'll show up and tempt you with the very thing you purposed to stop.

Thankfully, Jesus already gave us the example of how we should respond. Put the sword of the Spirit in your mouth and say, "It is written…." Speak the Word over your situation. When you do that, you'll free the Spirit of God to move on your behalf, supplying the power to get you through the test.

It doesn't matter what the temptation is; there's a scripture for it somewhere. Find it. Memorize it. Write it on a card. Hang it around your neck. Do whatever you need to do. Then when the temptation shows up, get the card out and speak the Word. Keep speaking it until you get the result Jesus got: "Then the devil left Him" (Matthew 4:11 NKJV).

Hang in there until Satan gives up. If you're serious about winning, he'll give up sooner than you think. And when you've successfully denied your flesh, God will be able to promote you according to His plan for your life.

Persecution for Jesus' Sake

The second kind of suffering Christians can expect to undergo is persecution.

Blessed are those who are persecuted for righteousness' sake, for theirs is the kingdom of heaven. Blessed are you when they revile and persecute you, and say all kinds of evil against you falsely for My sake. Rejoice and be exceedingly glad, for great is your reward in heaven, for so they persecuted the prophets who were before you (Matthew 5:10–12 NKJV).

The most important thing to note about this type of persecution is that it is persecution for Jesus' sake. Christians sometimes bring a different kind of persecution on themselves by not being smart in the way they approach unbelievers. They neglect common sense and ignore what Jesus said in Matthew 7:6: "Do not give what is holy to the dogs; nor cast your pearls before swine, lest they trample them under their feet, and turn and tear you in pieces" (NKJV). There are things between you and God that an unbeliever just won't understand. When you trot out your spirituality in front of unsaved friends and relatives, you're inviting persecution. It isn't for Jesus' sake. It's because you're acting foolishly, and the result is unnecessary hurt.

On the other hand, if you live your Christianity, you won't need to invite persecution. It will come on its own. The Word promises it.

Turn the Other Cheek

How do we respond when persecution comes for the sake of Christ? What do we do to survive it?

First of all, we can do what Matthew 5:12 tells us to do: "Rejoice, and be exceeding glad: for great is your reward in heaven."

Secondly, we can do what Matthew 5:39 says: "But I tell you not to resist an evil person. But whoever slaps you on your right cheek, turn the other to him also" (NKJV). This is part of the Sermon on the Mount that Jesus gave to His disciples. In it, He wasn't telling them how to let evil people take advantage of them but how to get the Gospel into the world. In other words, we're supposed to turn the other cheek when we're persecuted for sharing the Gospel—then and only then! We don't retaliate; we turn the other cheek.

Too often this verse has been lifted out of context and used to reinforce what I've already called the worm syndrome: "If you're going to be a Christian, you have to let the world walk on you. You can't defend your family or your property. You don't have any rights, and you can never stand up for yourself." I had this notion myself a long time, though I never liked it much. But it's plain from the rest of Scripture that God doesn't expect you to lie down and let Satan walk all over you.

If a burglar breaks into your house to molest your family and plunder your goods, what are you going to do? Ideally, you'll speak the Word of God in faith and he'll leave. But suppose you're a little backslidden—too much TV, maybe—and you don't have a whole lot of faith at the moment. When you say, "Be gone in the name of Jesus," and the burglar doesn't hear you, you'd better pick up a baseball bat and enforce the law yourself!

We need to realize that the only time we turn the other cheek is when it relates to persecution for the name of Jesus. Everywhere else in Scripture, the general principle is that we're to resist Satan, however he comes against us. When someone comes against us because of our stand for Christ, we don't defend ourselves, even if we're threatened with bodily harm. Why not? Because forbearance will get the best results from the lost. You'll be saying a whole lot more to them about God if you turn the other cheek than if you demonstrate how good a boxer you are.

Endurance vs. Deliverance

Let me remind you of one more point before we move on. A few chapters ago, I made the case that when physical harm is threatened during persecution for the name of Jesus, we have a choice whether to endure it or not. As explained in Hebrews 11:35, some believers chose martyrdom over deliverance and gave their lives for the Gospel. They could have chosen to escape the edge of the sword by faith, but because of the greater reward for accepting bodily harm, they welcomed it.

I believe that same option is available to us. If we are threatened with injury in promoting the Gospel, we have the option of using our faith to avoid it, even though submitting to "the edge of the sword" might be more effective.

It's a question we need to think about in advance, especially in these uncertain times. I've prayed about how I would react if my life was threatened because of my stand for the Lord. You may need to pray about it too. Make the choice while you have time, because if you wait until the last minute, you may make the wrong one.

In any case, the right kind of persecution means two things: you're living your Christianity in such a way that others recognize it, and you have a wonderful opportunity to change somebody's life for God. So when persecution comes, don't get offended, don't get hurt, don't feel rejected, and certainly don't take a swing. Do turn the other cheek, knowing that God is your recompense and that love never fails. And above all, rejoice, because you have an exceeding great reward.

The Suffering of Consecration

The first type of suffering Christians go through is resisting temptation. The second type is persecution for Jesus' sake. The third type of suffering is a broader self-denial called consecration, which we see Jesus employing in the Garden of Gethsemane.

> *And He was withdrawn from them about a stone's throw, and He knelt down and prayed, saying, "Father, if it is Your will, take this cup away from Me; nevertheless not My will, but Yours, be done." Then an angel appeared to Him from heaven, strengthening Him. And being in agony, He prayed more earnestly. Then His sweat became like great drops of blood falling down to the ground* (Luke 22:41–44 NKJV).

Jesus' flesh was far from eager to go to the Cross. But if He hadn't gotten a grip on His flesh, He would have turned the other way. And if He hadn't willingly submitted to the suffering that awaited Him, He would never have fulfilled God's highest purpose for His life.

The pattern is the same for us. Comprehensive self-denial may be the most difficult suffering we have to go through. But unless we deal with it properly, God can't take us into the highest reaches of His plan for us.

Imitating Jesus' Consecration

Very few of us will have to die on a cross, but there's a principle behind Jesus' submission to the cross that we need to understand clearly. Simply put, in order to continue maturing in Christ, we must consecrate our lives to the service of others. This is God's highest purpose for my life and yours.

Jesus is our example of this type of consecration. He laid down every ounce of self-interest in order to provide redemption for us, to open up before us an eternity in heaven and a higher quality of life on earth. In other words, He gave everything He had in order to bring us the Gospel.

As members of the body of Christ, we face the same challenge. How do we connect lost human beings with eternity in heaven and a higher quality of life here on earth? We do it by laying down all other priorities in order to take up the one God calls us to—getting the Gospel into other people's lives.

The focus of our lives shouldn't be our agenda, job, hobby, education, or kids. Our priority must be to connect other people with Jesus. Every other concern must bow to this one.

Typically, Christians serve when it's convenient. "Well, I'll join the ushers and serve once a week on Sunday." "I'll join the children's ministry and teach over the weekend." "I'll go evangelizing on Monday nights."

I'm grateful for ushers and teachers and Monday-night evangelists. But far too often, these things are done out of a sense of condemnation and as a guilty afterthought to the rest of the week. Modern Christianity has become a weekend affair. We serve a little bit here, a little bit there, but serve our own purposes the rest of the week. We show up on Sunday, serve God for an hour, and call it enough.

But it isn't. If we really want to experience God's highest and best, we're going to have to serve God's priorities all the time. As God sees it, we're on this earth for the purpose of bringing people to Jesus Christ. Everything we have including our time, money, talents, and other resources should be used to serve this purpose ahead of all others.

What About My Needs?

Our natural reaction, of course, is to look for a way out. We think, "Well, that's great, but if I'm serving everyone else, who will watch out for my needs?"

Scripture gives us a wonderful answer to this question. "But seek ye first the kingdom of God, and his righteousness; and all these things shall be added unto you" (Matthew 6:33).

"These things" are the goods of this world that people chase after. If you seek first the kingdom, you won't have to chase after them anymore. You won't have to worry about yourself, because God will take care of your every need. As you organize your life around His will and His plan, He'll take care of your life with spectacular generosity.

Most of us have never gone through this paradigm shift. Our flesh resists it with all its strength because when we follow His plan, everything we have belongs to God. All He has to do is say, "Give!" or "Do!" and we'll respond exactly as He wishes. And we do it because we know that He'll never abuse our trust or leave us high and dry after we've done what He requires.

Here's a test: would you clean out your bank account, sell everything you have, and give the proceeds to the Lord as Jesus required of the rich young ruler? Sure, the answer's easy if you haven't got anything in your bank account. The challenge comes when God has begun to prosper us, when the Word has started to work in our lives, and we've been blessed with a surplus. Prosperity tends to change people's view of reality. "Well, now, maybe God isn't telling me to give to Sister Sara's inner-city mission. Satan must be telling me to spend more money. Get thee behind me, Satan!"

Do you seriously think Satan would tell you to support the preaching of the Gospel?

We need to be brutally honest with ourselves about our priorities. Our lives are to be spent in the way Jesus spent His life—in the service of others.

The truth is, we can only accomplish this by consecration and prayer. And it's not a one-shot deal. We'll have to cope with self-centeredness on a daily basis, praying the prayer of consecration as Jesus did: "Not my will, Lord, but thine, be done."

This decision is hard to make and harder to act on. That's where the suffering comes in. But once we've done it, we'll be qualified for the highest purpose of God in our lives, and we'll experience God's best in return.

Walking Through Suffering

Remember, Christians don't have to suffer as Job did, but we are called to suffer as Jesus did, which includes:

- The suffering that comes from temptation: we're going to have to get a firm grip on our fleshly desires in order to move into God's plan for our lives.
- The suffering that comes from persecution: it will come as we live our lives for God. We respond by turning the other cheek, loving the offender, and rejoicing in the Lord.
- The suffering that comes from self-denial: we put other people's interests ahead of our own and begin to serve their needs.

The good news is that you don't have to walk through any of these sufferings on your own. The Holy Spirit stands ready to get you through them. You make the decision; He empowers it. And the same five steps that delivered Job from his sufferings are what will take you through the suffering of Jesus to maturity.

Step One

Have an unshakeable commitment to
God and His Word.

Step Two

Receive an authentic revelation of God
not based on hearsay.

Step Three

Repent of wrong words in addition to
wrong behavior.

Step Four

Forgive those who have offended you
and forget the offenses.

Step Five

Turn your attention and efforts to
serving others.

There's another final step we can apply to our lives
that wasn't available to Job. It's found in James 1:2–4:

My brethren, count it all joy when you fall into various
trials, knowing that the testing of your faith produces
patience. But let patience have its perfect work, that you
may be perfect and complete, lacking nothing (NKJV).

Count it all joy? That sounds strange. How can you
be joyful when you are struggling?

You can be joyful because you can look temptation in the
face and know that you don't have to give in. You know that
the joy of the Lord is your strength and that He will walk you
through whatever life brings your way. You know that if you
are patient and endure until the end, you'll become perfect
and mature, lacking nothing. You know that if you don't quit
(even in the toughest of circumstances), you will win.

Now that's something you can truly be joyful about.

Breezing Through the Storms of Life

Part 5

Facing the Storms of Life

There's one final element that is important to talk about regarding suffering. What do you do when you find yourself going through the same types of things that Job suffered—the things we don't have to go through? That's what I want to show you in this part of the book.

Just as Job was attacked by Satan with negative circumstances, we, too, will find ourselves facing negative circumstances in life—not the suffering we face as Christians, but rather what I like to refer to as "storms of life." Storms are unplanned events that hinder your progress toward the purpose of God. They take a lot of different forms including insufficiency, lack, sickness, disease, schism, division, oppression, depression. Any form of death that tries to enter your life is a storm intended to inhibit or stop progress in God's plan for your life.

The good news is that the Word of God plainly tells us how to breeze through any storm that comes our way. Take a look at what Jesus said in Matthew chapter 7:

Therefore whoever hears these sayings of Mine, and does them, I will liken him to a wise man who built his house on the rock: and the rain descended, the floods came, and the winds blew and beat on that house; and it did not fall, for it was founded on the rock. But everyone who hears these sayings of Mine, and does not do them, will be like a foolish man who built his house on the sand: and the rain descended, the floods came, and the winds blew and beat on that house; and it fell. And great was its fall (Matthew 7:24–27 NKJV).

Jesus was explaining two fundamental truths about life. First, storms come to everyone. Jesus didn't say "if" the rain comes or "if" the floods come. He plainly stated that storms will come. Storms come to every person simply because the enemy wants to stop the plan of God from becoming a reality in our lives.

The second truth we see from this passage of Scripture is that as we build our lives on the Word of God, the floods will not destroy us. Even more than that, they won't be able to shake us. Look how Luke 6:48 translates this part of the parable we read in Matthew 7:

...And when the flood arose, the stream beat vehemently against that house, and could not shake it, for it was founded on the rock (NKJV).

When you're faced with a storm and have founded your life upon the Word, the storm not only won't destroy you, but it won't even shake your house.

Many Christians assume they have built their lives on the Word because they have heard the Word and gained faith (Romans 10:17). But a good portion of those people still see their houses shaken when hit by the storms of life. Why? Contrary to what many people think, the basic issue isn't a lack of faith or knowledge. Jesus gives us the answer at the beginning of Matthew 7:24: "Therefore whoever hears these sayings of Mine, and does them..." (NKJV).

The key to breezing through the storms of life is "doing" the Word you have heard. This is the most common denominator in the Bible for how to live successfully.

Doesn't behavior automatically follow belief? you might be thinking. Well, not automatically. For example, I can know that an extra piece of pecan pie isn't good for me, but knowing that doesn't always stop me from eating it. James 2:20 says that faith without works is dead. The Word wouldn't have pointed this out if our actions always corresponded to our beliefs.

Don't get me wrong. Believing is necessary. I'm certainly not minimizing the importance of faith. But we must realize it isn't enough. We have to act on our faith.

Perhaps you're shaken about something in your life right now—sickness, depression, financial trouble, or relational division. Whatever the situation, stop and ask yourself, "Is there an area of my life in which I'm not doing the Word?" Because when you do the Word, you have the promise of not being shaken by the storms that life brings your way.

Become a Doer of the Word

James reiterates these truths in James 1:22–25:

But be doers of the word, and not hearers only, deceiving yourselves. For if anyone is a hearer of the word and not a doer, he is like a man observing his natural face in a mirror; for he observes himself, goes away, and immediately forgets what kind of man he was. But he who looks into the perfect law of liberty and continues in it, and is not a forgetful hearer but a doer of the work, this one will be blessed in what he does (NKJV).

The Bible is like a mirror. You really can't know who you are in Christ until you see yourself in the Word. There you'll see that you're healed, delivered, prosperous, and set free.

But you'll soon forget who you are in Christ if you hear these truths on Sunday and don't act on them on Monday. You won't remember that you are healed by the stripes of Jesus; you'll see the storm in the natural realm and base your decisions—and even your view of God—on the circumstances that you see. You must know who you are in Christ based on the direction of the Word and you must act on that knowledge.

What Exactly Are You Doing?

Sometimes people think they are doing the Word, when, in fact, they are acting on their own interpretation, not the Bible itself. For example, a friend of mine preached a sermon on healing one time. After the message was over, a lady from the congregation came up and threw her Bible on the podium and said, "It doesn't work." For a moment, they went back and forth arguing. He said, "It does work."

"It doesn't work," she replied.

"It does."

Eventually they got to the root of her problem. She had read James 5:14–15 where it says, "Is any sick among you? let him call for the elders of the church; and let them pray over him, anointing him with oil in the name of the Lord. And the prayer of faith shall save the sick, and the Lord shall raise him up; and if he have committed sins, they shall be forgiven him." This lady said, "I did that and I'm still sick. This stuff doesn't work."

My friend replied, "It does work," and they went back and forth again for a moment until he found out that the prayer of faith prayed over her went this way: "If it by Thy will, Lord, heal her."

That's not a prayer of faith—maybe a prayer of hope or wishful thinking, but certainly not faith. This lady was missing a vital element in following through on what that verse commanded her and the elders to do. She thought she was doing the Word, but she wasn't acting on the complete picture available.

The Word You've Heard

Some people may be thinking, *I don't know that much Word. I haven't been saved that long. Or I haven't studied the Word as much as Brother So-and-so. I'm never going to make it through the struggles in my life.*

Let me clarify something. You are responsible to do the Word that you've heard. If you haven't heard a certain Word preached or read about it in your Bible, you are not yet responsible for that Word. You are required to walk in the light you "have heard."

That doesn't mean you can slack off and not hear any more Word because you don't want to be responsible for it. If you let that happen, you'll run into the situation we see in Hosea 4:6: "My people are destroyed for lack of knowledge." But if you're making the effort to grow in God through reading your Bible, praying, and going to church, you don't need to be concerned about what you haven't heard. You're accountable to do the Word that you have heard. As you grow in God, you'll become accountable for more and more.

Don't Assume You Know the Answer

Another mistake Christians make is that they evaluate how well they're doing the Word by looking only at the part of their lives in which they're having trouble.

For example, if the storm is in the area of finances, Christians typically check their obedience to the Word in matters such as tithing or giving. The problem is that failure to do the Word in one element of the Christian life can leave us susceptible to storms in another. I've seen many people who are physically sick because of strife in a relationship. Others who are bogged down by unforgiveness have suffered financially. Don't make the mistake of deciding whether or not you're doing the Word by considering only the area of your life in which the crisis has come.

Be honest with yourself. If a storm is shaking you, the problem is not with God. Ask Him to show you in what area you're not doing the Word.

My own experience has been that when I make this request from a sincere heart, God will show me my mistake every time. I haven't always liked what He's said, and sometimes, I've even resisted it a little at first. But once I know where I'm missing it, I can make the necessary correction that will keep me from being shaken by the storm.

Don't Blame Others

There is one last thought about evaluating the storms in your life that you need to consider. You need to guard against the human tendency to shift responsibility for your circumstances onto others. Don't blame your troubles onto your boss, your spouse, your color, your socioeconomic background, or anything else. Accept full responsibility for the condition of your life and humble yourself enough to see where you haven't been doing the Word. Then you can say honestly to God, "Show me where I'm off. By the power of the Holy Spirit, I will make whatever changes are necessary." When you do this, you'll be positioned to walk in blessing, prosperity, and success.

Storms of Various Kinds

Storms come in all shapes and sizes. Identifying the type of storm you face is important, because you can then know if you need to alter your strategy during the storm. There are three main types of storms I want to show you.

Storms From Disobedience

Some people experience more storms than they really need to go through simply because they bring storms on themselves through disobedience—either failure to do the written Word or open resistance to what God speaks to their hearts through the Holy Spirit. For example, think about Jonah. He could have avoided a storm (not to mention three days in the belly of a fish) if he hadn't disobeyed God.

God doesn't bring storms to punish us or send Satan to teach us a lesson. But rebellion against God, whether through disobedience to God's Word or ignorance of God's instruction, will set us up for hard times.

How do we get through storms of this sort? The same way Jonah did. Repent! Our storm will then deposit us back onto the shore and we can go on with our lives.

Storms From Obedience

Someone once said that all you have to do to bring on a storm is either disobey or obey. There's certainly some truth in this statement because some storms come simply because we are obeying the will of God. For example, when Jesus told the disciples to cross the Sea of Galilee (Mark 4:35–41), they followed what He said and a storm nearly sank their ship. Were they doing something wrong and that's why the storm came? No. They were doing what Jesus asked them.

The enemy doesn't want you moving forward with God; he'll do anything he can to stop you from carrying out God's will for your life. Just as Jesus said in John 16:33, "In the world you will have tribulation; but be of good cheer, I have overcome the world" (NKJV).

How do you deal with this kind of storm? Use the command of faith as Jesus did: "Peace, be still." Speak the Word of God to your situation and then act on it. Jonah could have used the command of faith all day and it wouldn't have done him any good because his storm was the product of disobedience. But when you're in a storm that has come because of Satan's opposition to the will of God for your life, the command of faith will calm it.

Storms From Other People

Some storms come because of the people we're associated with. Paul experienced storms repeatedly for this reason. He wasn't doing anything wrong, but the people he was with were disobeying God. Look at the story of Paul's journey to Rome in Acts 27:9–44:

Now when much time had been spent, and sailing was now dangerous because the Fast was already over, Paul advised them, saying, "Men, I perceive that this voyage will end with disaster and much loss, not only of the cargo and ship, but also our lives." Nevertheless the centurion was more persuaded by the helmsman and the owner of the ship than by the things spoken by Paul (verses 9–11 NKJV).

The ship's owner wouldn't listen to Paul when he warned him not to leave Crete. Despite Paul's warning, they decided to make the trip. And what happened? They ended up sailing into a storm.

> But not long after, a tempestuous head wind arose, called Euroclydon. … And because we were exceedingly tempest-tossed, the next day they lightened the ship. On the third day we threw the ship's tackle overboard with our own hands. Now when neither sun nor stars appeared for many days, and no small tempest beat on us, all hope that we would be saved was finally given up (verses 14,18–20 NKJV).

Was it God's will that Paul was caught in this storm? Certainly not. But Paul, as a prisoner, didn't have an option. He could hardly choose to stay behind. The good news is that the Lord didn't abandon Paul just because he was caught in someone else's storm.

> But after long abstinence from food, then Paul stood in the midst of them and said, "Men, you should have listened to me, and not have sailed from Crete and incurred this disaster and loss. And now I urge you to take heart, for there will be no loss of life among you, but only of the ship. For there stood by me this night an angel of the God to whom I belong and whom I serve, saying, 'Do not be afraid, Paul; you must be brought before Caesar; and indeed God has granted you all those who sail with you.' Therefore take heart, men, for I believe God that it will be just as it was told me (verses 21–25 NKJV).

The Lord safely brought Paul through that storm, along with everyone else on board.

In Numbers 13–14, we see that Caleb and Joshua found themselves in the middle of a similar situation. Twelve spies were sent into the Promised Land to spy out what the Israelites would need to conquer in order to occupy the land. Ten of the men didn't see past the enemies who occupied the land; Joshua and Caleb did.

They believed God would help them possess the land. But sadly, they were the only ones.

The children of Israel listened to the bad report of the ten spies, and as a result, the whole nation of Israel wandered in the wilderness for forty years until most of them died there—all except Caleb and Joshua. They had to endure that forty-year delay because of the people they were with.

Here's one other example of this type of storm. Suppose you're in a marriage in which you're serving God but your spouse isn't. You don't need to repent because you haven't been disobeying God. The command of faith won't alter the situation, because your faith is for your life and you can't use your faith to impose your will on others.

What, then, do you do in this kind of storm? You endure. Endurance is the only way out of this kind of trial. God's grace will sustain you, as it did Paul, Caleb, and Joshua.

So when you face a storm, examine your life to determine what brought the storm. Ask the Lord to help you determine your course of action. If you've disobeyed, repent. If you haven't done anything wrong, use the command of faith. If you find yourself in a mess caused by someone else, ask God for the strength to endure.

And, through it all, be a doer of the Word.

Who You Are in Christ

Nobody likes the storms of life. Job didn't like it. His friends didn't like it. None of us like it when we find ourselves struggling to get rid of our fleshly desires and trying to obey God's commandments. That's why I'm grateful for the truth that Paul wrote in Colossians 1:26–27:

> The mystery which has been hidden from ages and from generations, but now has been revealed to His saints. To them God willed to make known what are the riches of the glory of this mystery among the Gentiles: which is Christ in you, the hope of glory (NKJV).

When you're born again, your spirit comes into union with God's Spirit. Christ is in you because you've been joined to Him; you've been made one spirit with Him. The two are welded together. This is what Paul meant when he said "Christ in you, the hope of glory."

If Christ is in you, then you have the solution to all your problems. Whatever you're suffering from, whatever storm you are going through, if you are born again, the answer lives in you.

Everything Job lacked—the new covenant, the promises of God, the Word of God, and the indwelling Holy Spirit—is wrapped up in this mystery. It is your hope of glory, your confidence that the covenant and promises of God are reliable, that the Word and the Spirit will bring you the better life that God wants you to have, now and forever.

Christ in you, you in Christ. The union is as close and complete as any union could possibly be.

The Vine and the Branches

Because of this wonderful mystery of Christ living in us, everything Jesus is, has, and ever had is available to us right now. Why? Because He is in us and we are vitally connected to the life available in and through Him. As Paul wrote in 1 Corinthians 3:21 and 23, "For all things are yours ... and ye are Christ's; and Christ is God's."

Jesus provided a great illustration of this in John 15. He likened Himself to a vine and us as the branches. Branches and vines share the same sap. The same sap that brings life to the vine runs through the branches that are attached to it.

In the same way, the life that flows through Christ (the vine) flows into His body (the branches). What is that life force? Something the Bible calls *zoë* life, which refers to "life as God has it."[1]

How does God have life? He has it infinitely, in every dimension—limitless life, free of sickness, disease, and lack, life that's filled with joy, peace, zeal, enthusiasm, and excitement. God's life is life at its fullest, and *zoë* is the God kind of life.

That life, *zoë* life, is what flows through you, a member of the body of Christ.

Because Christ lives in you, you not only have the same life, but you have the same power residing in you that Jesus did. As Jesus said in John 14:12, "He who believes in Me, the works that I do he will do also; and greater works than these he will do, because I go to My Father" (NKJV).

Jesus laid hands on the sick and they recovered. Jesus spoke and multiplied bread and fishes. That same Jesus is in you. When you lay hands on people, they will be healed. When you pray for a miracle of multiplication, you will see it because the same power that flows through Jesus flows through you.

The secret is to know who you are in Christ.

A Glorious Redemption

Who are you in Christ? Let's look at Romans 3:23–24, which makes the truth of our redemption clear:

For all have sinned and fall short of the glory of God, being justified freely by His grace through the redemption that is in Christ Jesus (NKJV).

When most of us consider "redemption," we don't think about it in any depth. We think of it as merely a legal transaction. But there's far more to it than that. By God's grace, we're redeemed from everything that Adam lost through disobedience. That's the glory of redemption.

We're redeemed from sickness and lack. We're redeemed from spiritual death and its consequences, now and eternally. We're redeemed from the curse of the Law. Deuteronomy 28:15–68 provides a very extensive definition of what is under the curse, and ultimately what we have been redeemed from. We've been redeemed from poverty, hunger, enemies, disease, insufficiency, anything bad you can think—and much worse!

The things we often ask God for are already ours under the new covenant. We seek healing, deliverance, financial soundness, mental health, as if they're kept in reserve somewhere and we have to pester God to get them. But the truth is, your redemption covers everything. It's yours because you've been brought into union with Jesus Christ, who is the Redeemer. The same life that flows through Him flows through you because you are in Christ Jesus.

New Creatures in Christ

Paul wrote in 2 Corinthians 5:17:

Therefore, if anyone is in Christ, he is a new creation; old things have passed away; behold, all things have become new (NKJV).

As we just read in Romans 3:24, we've been justified freely by His grace through the redemption that is in Christ Jesus. Therefore, the old things—the old poverty, the old sickness, the old mental and emotional turmoil, everything that has to do with sin and death—have passed away.

That doesn't mean there is an instant change in your physical makeup. If your hair is thinning before you get born again, you'll still have thin hair after you're saved. If you had blue eyes before you were saved, you will still have blue eyes after you accept Jesus into your life. Your outward condition isn't going to change automatically.

But your spirit, the real you, is recreated in the image and likeness of God almighty. You are a new creature in Christ, because you are in Christ. The old things are passed away and all things are become new.

What does this newness of life include?

Sufficiency

But my God shall supply all your need according to his riches in glory by Christ Jesus (Philippians 4:19).

All spiritual blessings

Blessed be the God and Father of our Lord Jesus Christ, who hath blessed us with all spiritual blessings in heavenly places in Christ (Ephesians 1:3).

Power

And what is the exceeding greatness of his power to us-ward who believe, according to the working of his mighty power, which he wrought in Christ, when he raised him from the dead, and set him at his own right hand in the heavenly places (Ephesians 1:19–20).

Dominion

And raised us up together, and made us sit together in the heavenly places in Christ Jesus (Ephesians 2:6 NKJV).

Triumph

Now thanks be to God who always leads us in triumph in Christ, and through us diffuses the fragrance of His knowledge in every place (2 Corinthians 2:14 NKJV).

This is only the beginning of what the Bible promises to us when we are "in Christ." More than a hundred other verses tell us who we are in Christ. The truth is that it doesn't matter how intimidating your situation looks or how many gloom-and-doom preachers try to convince you that you're stuck with it. The Bible says that if you're in Christ, you will always triumph. This is your birthright as a Christian.

This is why the Lord tells us in Philippians 4:13 that we can do all things through Christ. The only limit to God's activity in this earth is our willingness to find ourselves in Him.

How do you find yourself "in Him"? You do it by abiding in the vine. In the next chapter, I want to show you how to make "abiding in the vine" a practical reality for your life.

Abiding
in the Vine

You can stop struggling to make spiritual blessings surface in your life.

How? You do it by abiding in the Vine. In John 15:5, Jesus said, "I am the vine; ye are the branches: he that abideth in me, and I in him, the same bringeth forth much fruit: for without me ye can do nothing." If we abide in the Vine, spiritual fruit will come to the surface. We don't need to struggle to make it happen. In fact, as it says in John 15:8, the Father is glorified when our lives are filled with this spiritual fruit.

Let's go back to the beginning of John 15. This chapter truly is the essence of our walk with the Lord.

I am the true vine, and My Father is the vinedresser. Every branch in Me that does not bear fruit He takes away; and every branch that bears fruit He prunes, that it may bear more fruit. You are already clean because of the word which I have spoken to you. Abide in Me, and I in you. As the branch cannot bear fruit of itself, unless it abides in the vine, neither can you, unless you abide in Me. I am the vine, you are the branches. He who abides in Me, and I in him, bears much fruit; for without Me you can do nothing. If anyone does not abide in Me, he is cast out as a branch and is withered; and they gather them and throw them into the fire, and they are burned. If you abide in Me, and My words abide in you, you will ask what you desire, and it shall be done for you. By this My Father is glorified, that you bear much fruit; so you will be My disciples (John 15:1–8 NKJV).

In the natural, branches on a vine bear fruit. If we are branches abiding in Christ, we too must have the ability to bear fruit. But how?

Bearing fruit isn't some formula or method. It's not an eight-step plan we need to follow. Too many Christians feel like works-oriented formulas will produce godly faith in their lives, but they get so focused on their works that they forget about faith. They say something like, "I've got to jump out of bed tomorrow morning and confess fifty times before breakfast that I'm the righteousness of God in Christ." Spiritual calisthenics like this often have disappointing results, mainly because they don't come from the heart.

Don't get me wrong. Confession is important; it's something the Bible tells us to do. But we need to know what is ours in Christ before we can express it. Our confessions need to eventually flow from our hearts, not our heads.

Bearing fruit is actually very simple. It is the working out of spiritual truths in the natural realm. For example, your healing is already yours in Christ. It's a spiritual truth. When it manifests in the natural realm, it's called a fruit of the Spirit.

Most of you are probably thinking, *That's not one of the fruit of the Spirit!* You're right, it's not one of the spiritual qualities listed in Galatians 5:22–23, such as love, joy, peace, and patience. But any spiritual blessing that surfaces in the natural is fruit from your relationship of being in Christ. That includes every aspect of triumphant living, not only peace and joy, but freedom from sickness and poverty and relational disasters. This freedom comes when you are abiding in the Vine.

The Branches That Are Purged

You might have noticed something at the beginning of John 15 that trips people up—this idea of branches being purged. "Every branch in Me that does not bear fruit He takes away." When people read that, they're tempted to respond, "Whoops, I hope that's not me. I'd better get busy and bear some fruit or else I'll be in trouble."

If you profess Jesus as your Lord, you don't have to try to bear fruit—you will! You can't help it. An apple tree doesn't grunt and groan, hoping to get up the strength to pop out some fruit. Certainly not. Apples come forth because the tree is an apple tree. In the same way, you will bear fruit if you're living in Jesus.

Now you're not going to be laden with fruit the minute you're born again; there's a due season for any crop. Your fruit might start out simply as the fruit of repentance. From there, you'll grow and mature until you're a full-time fruit-bearer, just like an apple tree would.

What about the rest of verse two? It says, "And every branch that bears fruit He prunes, that it may bear more fruit." How many weird doctrines have sprung from that verse? "Oh, God's going to prune you back, brother; He's going to slice this away and snip that off, a little crisis here, a little disaster there."

At this point, you should know that's not the God we serve. So let's understand what this word for "prune" really means. In the Greek, it means "to cleanse."1 And in verse three of our text, Jesus tells us exactly how God does it: "Now ye are clean through the word which I have spoken unto you."

The Word of God cleanses us. We can see this confirmed in Ephesians 5:26, "That he might sanctify and cleanse [the Church] with the washing of water by the word." After you're born again and grafted into Christ, you begin bearing fruit. As you receive the Word of God, it continues to scrub your life clean, washing away the filth of the world that still clings to you. More and more, you find yourself doing the Word, bearing bigger and better fruit.

The key to the whole operation is abiding in Jesus.

Defining Abiding

What does abide mean? How do you abide in Jesus? The word can be defined as "to dwell,"[2] and the word *dwell* means "to live."[3] If you live in Jesus, you live for Him. He has first place in your thought life and daily activity. He is your priority.

It's a moment-by-moment decision. When your mind isn't taken up by your daily tasks of life such as housework or your job, let your thoughts turn toward the things of God. Maybe you'll want to pray in tongues. Set aside part of each day—the "firstfruits," perhaps—to be with God, study His Word, pray, focus your thoughts on Him. That's what abiding means.

Your leisure time, too, should be organized around Jesus. Certainly the Lord wants you to relax and enjoy yourself. But if you're abiding in Him, you won't be abiding in the evening news or the golf course or your collection of antiques.

When you get home from work, wouldn't it be profitable to kick off your shoes and pick up a good Word book or thumb through your Bible and read a little scripture instead of abiding in the TV set? The Bible's an exciting book, if you know where to look for what you need on a daily basis. It'll turn up your volume a lot louder than the eight o'clock movie.

Maybe that seems a little fanatical to you. Well, too many Christians are fanatical about things that will only produce death in their lives. I offer no apology for being fanatical about things that produce the God kind of life for me.

The good news is that this "fanatical" commitment is all we are responsible for. Abiding in Jesus is done from a position of spiritual rest. You can walk away from your struggles and put all your formulas in the drawer, scrap all the little deals you've been trying to work up with God. The Bible says that if you abide in Him, you will bear much fruit—all the fruit that Job and the Old Testament saints struggled to bear, and much more besides.

When the things that are in you because you are in Christ begin to rise to the surface, you'll step out in triumph. You'll start prospering according to His riches in glory. You'll begin enjoying your redemption from the curse of sickness. You'll see yourself breeze through the storms and sufferings that life brings your way. You'll start bearing the other fruits of the Spirit—love, joy, peace, patience, etc. You won't have to work them up. They'll just rise to the surface because they are fruit of the Spirit working in your life.

Keep an eye on your fruit-bearing progress. Use some of the quick checks I've pointed out in this book to see whether you're abiding or not: commit to God, have your own revelation of Him, repent of wrong words and behavior, forgive and forget, serve others. In other words, do the Word.

But above all, remember that these things can be accomplished without a struggle because of who you are in Christ, if you will just—abide in the Vine!

Conclusion

Suffering is an often misunderstood concept that people easily blame God for. But as you saw in the truths presented in this book, God never intended for us to suffer through life. He has a bigger picture, a better plan for us to carry out. Suffering is not part of that plan.

Satan wants to keep people in the dark as long as possible about the suffering question. The more people blame God, the less they blame Satan, and the more they allow suffering to be a part of their lives.

I'm thankful we can live in the entire light that the Bible presents. We don't need to be caught in the undertow of the world's way of thinking regarding suffering. We can recognize who God is, who our enemy is, and who we are because of Christ.

The next time you hear someone talking about the struggles of Job or Paul's thorn in the flesh, pat them on the back and say, "Did you know we don't need to struggle as Job did?" Invite them to coffee and walk them through the truths presented in this book. Show them how to answer the question that too many people get tripped up on: Does God really make people suffer?

Now you know that you can confidently answer, "No, He doesn't."

Endnotes

Chapter 2

1. *Dictionary.com Unabridged (v 1.1),* s.v. "confusion." http://dictionary.reference.com/browse/confusion (accessed: June 26, 2008).
2. Strong, "Greek," entry #1515, p. 25.

Chapter 3

1. *Merriam-Webster's Collegiate Dictionary,* 11th ed., s.v. "patient."
2. Strong, "Greek," entry #5281, p. 74.

Chapter 5

1. Thomson, 827. Available online at: http://thetencommandmentsministry.us/ ministry/charles_thomson/job_psalms.pdf.
2. Strong, "Greek," entry #769, p. 16.

Chapter 7

1. Strong, "Greek," entry #3985, p. 56.

Chapter 15

1. Vine, s.v. "life," p. 218.

Chapter 16

1. Strong, "Greek," entry #2508, p. 38.
2. Strong, "Greek," entry #3306, p. 47.
3. *Merriam-Webster's Collegiate Dictionary,* 11th ed., s.v. "dwell."

References

Dictionary.com Unabridged (v 1.1), Random House, Inc.

Merriam-Webster's Collegiate Dictionary, 11th ed. Springfield: Merriam-Webster, Incorporated, 2007.

Strong, James. *Abingdon's Strong's Exhaustive Concordance of the Bible.* "Greek Dictionary of the New Testament." Nashville: Abingdon Press, 1890.

Thomson, Charles. *The Holy Bible, containing the Old and New Covenant, commonly called the Old and New Testament: translated from the Greek.* Philadelphia: Jane Aitken, 1808.

Vine, W.E. *Vine's Concise Dictionary of the Bible.* Nashville: Thomas Nelson, Inc. 2005.

Prayer of Salvation

A born again, committed relationship with God is the key to a victorious life. Jesus, the Son of God, laid down His life and rose again so that we could spend eternity with Him in heaven and experience His absolute best on earth. The Bible says, "For God so loved the world, that he gave his only begotten Son, that whosoever believeth in him should not perish, but have everlasting life" (John 3:16).

It is the will of God that everyone receive eternal salvation. The way to receive this salvation is to call upon the name of Jesus and confess Him as your Lord. The Bible says, "That if thou shalt confess with thy mouth the Lord Jesus, and shalt believe in thine heart that God hath raised him from the dead, thou shalt be saved. ...For whosoever shall call upon the name of the Lord shall be saved" (Romans 10:9, 13).

Jesus has given salvation, healing, and countless benefits to all who call upon His name. These benefits can be yours if you receive Him into your heart by praying this prayer:

Heavenly Father, I come to You admitting that I am a sinner. Right now, I choose to turn away from sin, and I ask You to cleanse me of all unrighteousness. I believe that Your Son, Jesus, died on the cross to take away my sins. I also believe that He rose again from the dead so that I may be justified and made righteous through faith in Him. I call upon the name of Jesus Christ to be the Savior and Lord of my life. Jesus, I choose to follow You, and I ask that You fill me with the power of the Holy Spirit. I declare right now that I am a born again child of God. I am free from sin and full of the righteousness of God. I am saved in Jesus' name, amen.

If you have just received Jesus Christ as your Savior, or if this book has changed your life, we would like to hear from you. Please write us at:

Mac Hammond Ministries
PO Box 29469
Minneapolis, Minnesota 55429-2946

You can also visit us on the web at:

mac-hammond.org

About The Author

Mac Hammond is senior pastor of Living Word Christian Center, a large and growing body of Christian believers in Brooklyn Park (a suburb of Minneapolis), Minnesota. He is the host of the *Winner's Way* broadcast and author of several internationally distributed books. Mac is broadly acclaimed for his ability to apply the principles of the Bible to practical situations and the challenges of daily living.

Mac Hammond graduated from Virginia Military Institute in 1965 with a Bachelor's degree in English. Upon graduation, he entered the Air Force with a regular officer's commission and reported for pilot training at Moody Air Force Base in Georgia. He received his wings in November 1966, and subsequently served two tours of duty in Southeast Asia, accumulating 198 combat missions. He was honorably discharged in 1970 with the rank of Captain.

Between 1970 and 1980, Mac was involved in varying capacities in the general aviation industry including ownership of a successful air cargo business serving the Midwestern United States. A business acquisition brought the Hammonds to Minneapolis where they ultimately founded Living Word Christian Center in 1980 with 12 people in attendance.

After more than 28 years, that group of twelve people has grown into an active church body of more than 9,000 members. Today some of the outreaches that spring from Living Word include Maranatha Christian Academy, a fully-accredited, pre-K through 12th grade Christian school; Maranatha College, an evening college with an uncompromising Christian environment; Living Free Recovery Services, a state licensed outpatient treatment facility for chemical dependency; The Wells at 7th Street, a multi-faceted outreach to inner-city residents; CFAITH, an online cooperative missionary outreach of hundreds of national and international organizations providing faith-based content; and a national and international media outreach that includes hundreds of audio/video teaching series, the *Winner's Way* broadcast, the *PrayerNotes* newsletter, and the *Winner's Way* magazine.

Other Books

By Mac Hammond

Angels at Your Service
Releasing the Power of Heaven's Host

Doorways to Deception
How Deception Comes, How It Destroys, and
How You Can Avoid It

Following the Fire
Discovering How God Leads You
by the Desires of Your Heart

Heirs Together
Solving the Mystery of a Satisfying Marriage

The Last Millennium
A Revealing Look at the Remarkable
Days Ahead and How You Can Live
Them to the Fullest

Living Safely in a Dangerous World
Keys to Abiding in the Secret Place

Plugged In and Prospering
Embracing the Spiritual Significance and Biblical
Basis for the Local Church

Positioned for Promotion
How to Increase Your Influence and Capacity to
Lead

Real Faith Never Fails
Detecting (and Correcting) Four
Common Faith Mistakes

Simplifying Your Life
Divine Insights to Uncomplicated Living

Soul Control
Whoever Controls Your Soul,
Controls Your Destiny

By Mac Hammond (continued)

Water, Wind, & Fire
Understanding the New Birth and the Baptism of the Holy Spirit

Water, Wind, & Fire—The Next Steps
Developing Your New Relationship With God

The Way of the Winner
Running the Race to Victory

Who God Is Not
Exploding the Myths About His Nature and His Ways

Winning In Your Finances
How to Walk God's Pathway to Prosperity

Winning Your World
Becoming a Person of Influence

Yielded and Bold
How to Understand and Flow With the Move of God's Spirit

By Mac and Lynne Hammond

Keys to Compatibility
Opening the Door to a Marvelous Marriage

By Lynne Hammond

Dare to Be Free!

Heaven's Power for the Harvest
Be Part of God's End-Time Spiritual Outpouring

Living in the Presence of God
Receive Joy, Peace, and Direction
in the Secret Place of Prayer

Love and Devotion
Prayer Journal

The Master Is Calling
Discovering the Wonders of
Spirit-Led Prayer

The Master Is Calling Workbook
Discovering the Wonders of
Spirit-Led Prayer

Renewed in His Presence
Satisfying Your Hunger for God

Secrets to Powerful Prayer
Discovering the Languages of the Heart

Staying Faith
How to Stand Until the Answer Arrives

The Table of Blessing
Recipes From the Family and Friends of Living
Word Christian Center

When Healing Doesn't Come Easily

When It's Time for a Miracle
The Hour of Impossible Breakthroughs
Is Now!

Whispers From the Secret Place
A 31-day Journey